HOW TO CREATE
CALM DINING HALLS

How to Create Calm Dining Halls by Jenny Mosley

First published in 2015 by:
Positive Press Ltd
28A Gloucester Road
Trowbridge
Wiltshire   BA14 0AA

Telephone: 01225 719204
Fax: 01225 712187
E-mail: positivepress@jennymosley.co.uk
Website: www.circle-time.co.uk

ISBN 978-1-904866-67-1

Printed in the UK by www.heronpress.co.uk

Contents

Foreword

Why I wrote this book

Acknowledgements

How to use this book

Foreword

It was a pleasure to be asked to write a foreword for Jenny Mosley's new book. I believe it's the first book to focus solely upon dining halls.

My career has focused clearly and passionately upon improving the food and nutrition of children at lunchtime in schools. It was a privilege to work with Jamie Oliver to bring the whole issue of healthy eating to public attention. Jenny too has worked endlessly for the last thirty years to try to improve dining hall systems and playgrounds, so together we have fantastic ideas to make lunchtimes and playtimes as healthy, organised and enjoyable as they can be for children. Let's face it, lunchtime is a very important part of the school day.

As a keen campaigner for the improvement of children's school lunches, I can see how improving the children's perceptions about food, the nutritional aspects and presentation of food, is vital in helping children learn how to make healthy choices and enjoy balanced meals. I can also see how sometimes the dining hall systems themselves let down this process.

I am very familiar with the dining hall scenario where children are queuing for a long time and their behaviour slips, noise levels rise and after that nobody can enjoy their lunch. Some children struggle to understand the menu choices, or are worried about trying new foods. There are many ideas that schools can implement to help make the school dining experience a happy, healthy and peaceful time, so that children can sit and enjoy their lunch in a sociable way in calm and pleasant surroundings, and importantly, this can be done without a huge budget to spend on improving everything.

In my experience it is vital for the catering staff and midday supervisory assistants to work together as a team, to have meetings and talk to each other and with other members of school staff.

Both Jenny Mosley and I advocate the use of a "Whole School Approach" to positive lunchtimes and this book helps to bring many of these ideas together, to involve everyone and to facilitate the work of the lunchtime catering staff and midday supervisors.

So, good luck with improving your dining halls and I am really pleased to see progress being made in this important area for children alongside the work and campaigning on the nutritional aspects of dining that many of us care so deeply about.

Jeanette Orrey, MBE
Former School Catering Manager.
Author *The Dinner Lady: Change The Way Your Children Eat Forever*, and *Second Helpings*.
Co-founder of the Food for Life Partnership.
School Meals Policy Advisor to the Soil Association.
Expert Member of the Government "School Food Plan" Panel.

Why I wrote this book

I have been working in education as a teacher since 1972. In the 1980s I was asked by Wiltshire LA to work in their schools promoting the listening system of "Circle Time", which culminated in my first book *All-Round Success* (WEST Publications, 1987). I was then asked by many other LAs and headteachers to visit their schools to promote listening and positive behaviour. I therefore listened, through Circle Time, to many children, teachers and midday supervisors and became aware of how their experiences in dining halls were one of the key factors helping to shape attitudes and behaviour in schools. I always insisted therefore that I visited a school's dining hall and playground, so I could afterwards run a Circle Time for midday supervisors, teaching assistants, and if possible, catering assistants, to focus on the problems and the potentials together. These experiences are highlighted in my second best-selling book *Turn Your School Round* (LDA, 1993).

Ever since then, as part of my whole school training and consultancy, I have been visiting dining halls in tiny rural schools, large inner city schools and vast international schools! My mind feels steeped in the very best and worst of practices. Finally, having spent the last two decades promoting listening and speaking for adults and children, I really wanted to write a book devoted just to dining halls.

The truth is that midday supervisors have historically been treated badly by education. Currently most of them are on the minimum wage. Some schools have managed to employ teaching assistants or play leaders to cover all their dining hall, lunchtime and playground duties, but many more still have teams of mostly women who are poorly paid, have had no training in the job and sometimes are expected to stay for meetings unpaid. We would love to fight the battle that promotes these people and this whole area of education, but it is a political one – so in this book I am just going to concentrate on the key issues we can help with.

The dining hall experience can drain or boost everyone's energy. It can be the most difficult and unhappy experience for everyone, or it could be the one time in the day where children and adults relax, enjoy each other's company and eat well to give themselves a physical boost ready for the challenging afternoons!

Jenny Mosley

P.S. I'm not an expert, but I am an enthusiast!

Acknowledgements

This book has been a joy to write, because along the way I have been to some wonderful schools with brilliant dining halls, and I have met some of the most creative and inspiring staff ever! I cannot individually name everyone that has inspired me but I would like to thank the following:

All the wonderful schools that I am constantly invited into and the staff I meet during my training who have provided us with so much dining hall inspiration!

Headteacher, John Talbot and Unit Catering Manager, Juliet Underwood, at Smith's Wood Primary Academy, Solihull, for allowing me to share in their well-run dining hall experiences, documenting their practices and taking beautiful photographs for the book to inspire us all.

Headteacher, Michael Dillon and class teacher, Sarah Waight, at Kew Riverside Primary School, Richmond, for believing in a better vision for school lunchtimes and playtimes, and for being very inclusive by using their school to host training courses that allow many other local schools to be inspired too.

Ian Read, a wonderful headteacher at Watercliffe Meadow Community Primary School, Sheffield – one of the schools that has received my Gold Award – his whole staff team (it's a big school) have embraced the Golden Model and have gone from strength to strength by creating amazing learning environments in the classrooms, playground and dining hall. Your Meadow Café school dining hall photograph on page 39 will get people talking!

Jeanette Orrey, MBE, who kindly took time out of her busy life to write the foreword for this book. We are totally in awe of Jeanette, who has channelled a huge amount of energy into campaigning, improving school meals and raising awareness around children's food and eating habits. Thank you from adults and children everywhere!

Jamie Oliver, a national treasure, for motivating millions of us with his zest for life and his imaginative and creative use of good wholesome food. Most importantly his commitment to getting schools to think and act differently is working.

We are still very impressed by those local authorities that are managing to keep their "Healthy School" teams in these cash strapped times. They do a wonderful job helping schools to keep focused on physical and emotional wellbeing through very practical ideas. They co-ordinate and disseminate research which schools could otherwise be too busy to notice. We need to keep these teams going across the UK.

A big thank you must go to Nick Bolton, Wiltshire Healthy Schools Co-ordinator, who immediately gave us knowledge, support, and most importantly, enthusiasm when we needed it.

Hampshire Healthy Schools, who have a huge remit and are thriving! Ian Wright, the Healthy Schools Officer, invited me to speak at their training day on "Universal Free School Meals, Dining Halls and Improving Lunchtimes". They are working very strategically with schools and motivating them with practical support and a range of excellent resources. We will be working more closely with Glynis Wright and her HIAS, Education and Inclusion Team in the future and with HC3S, Hampshire's caterers, who continue to champion the whole school approach to school meals while serving 70,000 meals a day!

Headteacher, Matthew O'Brien and the staff at Birchgrove Primary School, Swansea for allowing us to reproduce their lovely "Golden Table" photograph.

The Food Dudes for their pioneering strategies, that can be seen in their pilot schools to motivate children to eating more healthily; especially fruit and vegetables. Schools are excited by what they bring to the table!

My friend and colleague Helen Sonnet for helping me to brainstorm ideas and to get us started on the whole project.

Andy Garrett, who worked his design magic on this book – although, rightly, he has told us that next time we must give him more time so he can be even more creative!

Clare Mortimer, who stepped in at the last minute with good-natured calmness to "tweak" the book.

Sam Ryder, Claire Tolladay and the rest of the team at Heron Press UK, Birmingham, who are always being asked by us to do the impossible by bringing books to print again and again with huge time constraints. They do it with a wry smile and good hearts.

Finally, to my own team ...

I would like to say a big thank you to Sheila McClurg, our Positive Press editor, who has done a sterling job with this book and who has been creatively involved at every stage. We need her rigour and ability to tenaciously complete tasks. She has been a great asset to this book and there has been nothing slow and measured about bringing it to fruition! It's been a bounding "Let's get this book written now!" type of approach – an editor's nightmare – and not one we'll ever repeat! Promise!

Jack Austen, our former in-house designer, was a joy to work with. Thank you for all your design input over the years and helping Sheila with all the resources in the book. You have an ability to interpret my ideas when I can't even articulate them properly, a great eye for detail and, best of all, a really pleasant calm nature.

This book would be nowhere without Zara! Dr Zara Niwano, – let's give Zara her full title today – has worked with me over many years. She's a great researcher, a tenacious hunter-gatherer of ideas, research and initiatives and a believer in me, as well as being the most patient, kind, gentle person you could ever meet. She just lives the Golden Rules naturally.

How to use this book

We have tried to make this book as simple as possible for busy teachers and staff in schools and for those with tired eyes! So this is what we have done to try to make things bright, interesting and clear:

➢ The main written text is on the right-hand side of the page.

➢ Certain comments from the right-hand side text have been magnified slightly and put in the left-hand margin so you can see these at a glance.

➢ We have used the terms "midday supervisor", "lunchtime supervisor" and "dining hall supervisor" interchangeably, unless otherwise stated, because schools vary so widely in how they refer to these important people! "Catering staff", of course, refers to the equally important staff who actually manage, prepare and serve the food.

➢ We have included some great case studies so that you can read what other people have done.

➢ There are some lovely photographs to add some colour and inspiration to your thinking.

➢ At the very back of the book (in appendices 1 and 2) you will find lots of photocopiable dining hall questionnaires and resources.

➢ There is also a free CD-ROM of the "Photocopiable Material" and the questionnaires. The questionnaires are customisable so you can change the questions to suit your school or situation. Please print them off or save them on your PCs/MACs for later use. The resources can be printed or copied as many times as you want, within your school (they are not for sale or distribution outside your school).

➢ Where there is a relevant resource to accompany a suggestion in the text, we have added an easy to understand symbol in the margin – please see "Key to resources" on page 16.

Key to resources

We have a resource to help you with this. Please visit our web shop at www.circle-time.co.uk/shop.

A customisable and printable questionnaire is available on the free CD-ROM that comes with this book (there are also photocopiable versions in the back of this book). Feel free to print these resources as they are, or customise to suit your specific needs!

You will find these printable/photocopiable resources on the CD-ROM and in Appendix 2 at the back of this book. Feel free to print and photocopy them for your school!

Chapter 1
Do any of these scenarios ring true for you?

Headteacher

I do wish that more staff would eat their lunches with the children. I did make this suggestion a few months ago, but very few staff had opted to do this. I'm reluctant to try and push this one, as the staff would complain that they needed time out away from the children to recover. I know, though, that it would be great for the children and adults to eat together; they would actually come to enjoy the more relaxed atmosphere away from the classrooms where they could chat to each other. It would also allow the children to see their teachers in a different light and help to build positive relationships. How to persuade them – that is the question. Even with two sittings, the dining hall is still crammed to capacity. No wonder there are so many collisions and so much food is dropped onto the floor. Universal free school meals are the last straw, as I have to stand in the hall every day hurrying everyone along all lunchtime!

Universal free school meals are the last straw as I have to stand in the hall every day hurrying everyone along all lunchtime!

Dining hall supervisor

I had all sorts of great ideas to improve lunchtimes, from the introduction of staggered sittings, to improving the look of the dining hall, as at the moment it is a bit dreary and shabby. I was sure that if it was re-painted and had attractive pictures on the walls, wipe-clean cloths on the tables and was generally made to look more inviting, the children would enjoy eating here much more. Changing the queuing system and introducing a whole school approach to behaviour would make all the supervisors' jobs easier, so why is everyone too busy and negative to make it happen? Either it is "too expensive" or "too difficult" to organise or enforce. Everyone always seems to be against any kind of change even when the long-term benefits are obvious!

Changing the queuing system, introducing a whole school approach ... would make all the supervisors' jobs easier, so why is everyone too busy and negative to make it happen?

Midday supervisor

Oh, now I can feel another headache coming on. I've only been a midday supervisor for a month, but it isn't at all how I hoped it to be. I had been so looking forward to working with children now that my own youngest has started school. This job fitted in so well with the times when I am free to work and seemed ideal – now I'm not so sure. I could never have believed the blast of noise in the hall. Two hundred children in one go, all talking and jostling at once, the senior supervisor shouting at the top of her voice to make herself heard, children pushing and shoving – even past her. Sometime she blows a whistle! So much food on the tables and on the floor. They take very little notice of anything that I ask them to do and are even rude to me sometimes.

Dining hall caterer

I really need all my patience when I'm serving the children. Some of them look at the vegetables and fruit as if they were alien beings! It's obvious that they have never seen them before, but I'm sure that if they were given the chance to taste them, most of the children would enjoy the different flavours and textures. Plus, they would be a great introduction to healthier eating. Maybe we could display the food more attractively to make it look really appetising and tempt the children to try something different? But we never have meetings. We don't seem to be part of the school.

Child

That was the bell for lunchtime! I hate that sound most of all. Everyone pushes me in the queue. I can never find a seat by someone I know. Most of all I hate opening my lunch box in front of all the others. They always look at my food and talk about everything in my lunch box, making so called "funny" comments about the food and pretending to be sick. My mum always makes me a healthy lunch, but the food she gives me makes everyone crowd round and have a laugh. So now I leave things in my lunch box and don't eat them. Still, it is better to feel hungry than be laughed at.

Two hundred children in one go, all talking and jostling at once, the senior supervisor shouting at the top of her voice to make herself heard, children pushing and shoving …

I really need all my patience when I'm serving the children. Some of them look at the vegetables and fruit as if they were alien beings!

Mum always makes me a healthy lunch, but the food she gives me makes everyone crowd round and have a laugh. So now I leave things in my lunch box.

Child

I feel really nervous going into the dining hall. I have looked at the names of the meals on the menu for today, but I don't understand what they mean. As usual, the children behind me are pushing and getting cross as I try and work out what I want to choose. I just hope I don't choose something horrible by mistake, like yesterday.

Parent

I'm never sure about lunchtimes at our school. My son prefers a packed lunch, but he complains that he can't sit with all his friends as they have hot lunches. He seems to rush his lunch so he can get out to the playground more quickly. My daughter really likes her school lunches, but she says she has to wait for too long in a queue and then when she has her lunch she says it's just too noisy for her when she is trying to eat. I think lunchtime should be a really nice time for both of them but it's just not working.

As usual, the children behind me are pushing and getting cross as I try and work out what I want to choose.

My son prefers a packed lunch , but he can't sit with all his friends as they have hot lunches. He seems to rush his lunch so he can get out to the playground more quickly.

Chapter 2
Why do you need this book?

"Inspectors must ensure that they observe pupils in a range of situations outside normal lessons to evaluate other aspects of behaviour and safety, for example during lunchtime, including in the dining hall, and break or play times" (Ofsted, 2014).

You need this book if:

You need this book if the children in your dining hall are not happy and calm.

➢ Any of the previous scenarios touch a nerve.
➢ The children in your dining hall are not happy and calm.
➢ Children experience high levels of noise, unfairness, shouting, long queues, pushing in the lines, poor food and a sense of rush which then hypes them up into a really anxious, cross or withdrawn state.
➢ You want to promote the social skills associated with dining with others.
➢ You would like to offer the social experiences of collecting and eating food whilst engaging with others in a positive way.
➢ You are really keen for the children and staff in your school to enjoy sociable, enjoyable lunchtimes.
➢ You want your children to be focused, calm, happy and ready to learn after their lunchtime.

What does research tell us?

"Improving the dining environment and the nutritional quality of the food over a twelve week period positively impacted upon learning-related behaviours in children" (School Food Trust, 2010).

Research in the last few years has shown a positive link between improving the dining experience and positive learning behaviour. One study, by the School Food Trust (2010) – now the Children's Food Trust – found that "improving the dining environment and the nutritional quality of the food over a twelve week period positively impacted upon learning-related behaviours in children". After the intervention, researchers found that in the afternoons, pupils were "over three times more likely to be 'on-task' working and were more alert".

Encouraging healthy eating

The link between pupil health and wellbeing and attainment has already been established.

The link between pupil health and wellbeing and attainment has already been established. "Promoting physical and mental health in schools creates a virtuous circle reinforcing children's attainment and achievement that in turn improves their wellbeing, enabling children to thrive and achieve their full potential" (Brooks 2013).

Efforts to encourage healthy eating in schools have been shown to have a really positive effect.

Encouraging healthy eating has become an important factor in improving the school dining experience and children's health. A rise in childhood obesity and other weight-related conditions threatens the wellbeing of some pupils. Efforts to encourage healthy eating in schools have been shown to have a really positive effect. The Food Dudes (an educational programme to encourage healthy eating involving behavioural strategies and fun activities, see p.68), found that after their unique encouragement intervention programme, 100% more children chose to eat at least one portion of fruit; 192% more children ate vegetables and 36% fewer children ate unhealthy snacks (Food Dudes, 2014).

There is evidence that the children in Jamie Oliver's "Feed me better" school food campaign behaved better and achieved more in class (Belot and James, 2009).

There is evidence that the children in Jamie Oliver's "Feed me better" school food campaign behaved better and achieved more in class following a school food intervention programme introducing more nutritious school lunches. In Greenwich, where the campaign began, research revealed that English and Science test results rose significantly among 11-year olds and absenteeism owing to sickness fell. The report's researchers say the positive effects of this on educational attainment are "comparable in magnitude" to those seen after the introduction of the "literacy hour" in the 1990s (Belot and James, 2009).

"A whole school approach, embracing the school curriculum as well as the food and drink available in schools, is very important to providing good nutrition." (Weichselbaum and Buttriss, 2014).

The National Diet and Nutrition Survey (NDNS) found that, "a whole school approach, embracing the school curriculum as well as the food and drink available in schools, is very important to providing good nutrition" (Weichselbaum and Buttriss, 2014).

Creating the right ambience, implementing efficient systems and creating a positive experience in your dining hall involves taking a close look at, and possible re-evaluation of, all of the current practices relating to dining, healthy eating and lunchtimes within your school. To help start this process off, we have included some trigger questions for headteachers, teachers and teaching assistants, midday supervisors and catering staff, children and parents (see Chapter 3 and Appendix 1).

How can this book help you?

This book can help create a lunchtime dining experience that is:

➢ In a welcoming and inviting dining space.
➢ Accompanied by a calm and peaceful atmosphere that feels safe and secure.
➢ Enjoyable and relaxing for children and adults to sit and eat together.
➢ Efficient and well-organised.
➢ Considerate of the needs of everyone involved.
➢ Encouraging good manners and positive social skills.
➢ Based on high behavioural expectations.
➢ Following calm and efficient systems.
➢ Taking the best of what you have and making it run more smoothly and efficiently after thinking things through and taking action.

This is what we cannot do in this book

Although the following issues are important for happy and healthy children at lunchtimes, we cannot help you change these elements of the dining hall:

➢ The physical environment and equipment in your dining hall and kitchens.
➢ The quality, quantity or arrangements for the food that is bought in.
➢ Menus and ideas for healthy, nutritious foods.
➢ The funding for school meals.
➢ Staffing issues.

We can only offer advice and point you in the right direction. At the end of the book we have tried carefully to signpost you to some relevant authorities and initiatives (see Chapter 11).

This book can help create a lunchtime dining experience that is efficient and well-organised.

At the end of the book we have tried carefully to signpost you to some relevant authorities and initiatives.

Chapter 3
The only way forward is a whole school approach

The very best way to create a successful and happy dining hall is to adopt a whole school approach.

To get an overall view, you really need to ask everyone for their opinions and suggestions.

The very best way to create a successful and happy dining hall is to adopt a whole school approach. If everyone involved has a say, they are more likely to make the system work, feel respected and involved, and have a sense of ownership, which will make any systems work better.

To get an overall view, you really need to ask everyone for their opinions and suggestions. You will gain an overall impression of what is and is not currently working well and may find some of the suggestions are innovative and helpful in making the changes and improvements.

To achieve an all-round view of the dining experience, you need to speak to:

➢ Headteachers
➢ Teaching staff
➢ Governors and parents or carers
➢ Midday supervisors and catering staff
➢ Children

The intensity, the noise, the lack of time, the range of problems, the safety guidelines – the list is so endless!

Often when people are looking at their dining hall experience, no one knows quite where to start. The intensity, the noise, the lack of time, the range of problems, the safety guidelines – the list is so endless it can overwhelm people.

Collect together all the different views and they will come under various headings.

The first thing to do is check how everyone is feeling about the dining hall. Collect together all the different views and they will come under various headings. All the headings point you to systems that aren't working properly and whatever system most stakeholders are flagging up is probably the one you need to start with first. To help with this, I have created some trigger questions for you to ask the different stakeholder groups. Examples of these trigger questions follow on pages 27-33, and are also included in the photocopiable questionnaires in Appendix 1 at the back of this book. As every school is unique, I would suggest that you adapt, add in or delete some of these questions to suit your particular situation (these trigger questions also appear in the customisable questionnaires on the accompanying CD-ROM – so you can tailor the questionnaires to suit your school).

Some schools put a "post box" in their reception area or hall so that responses to the questionnaire can be posted anonymously and sometimes you get a more honest set of answers! Circle Times are great for getting ideas from pupils.

Some schools put a "post box" in their reception area or hall so that responses to the questionnaire can be posted anonymously.

Trigger questions for headteachers

○ What is not working well in your dining hall, e.g. are queues too long? Is the noise too loud? Is there waste food lying on the tables and under them?

○ Are you having to spend a large part of every day in the dining hall helping out?

○ Have "Universal free school meals" tipped the balance into chaos?

○ Have you noticed some children not eating?

○ Are there comments from parents/carers or staff about children crying at lunchtime?

○ Is there enough time for the children to sit and eat?

○ How is your dining hall organised and is there anything in the physical environment that you can see not working?

○ Do teachers release the children on time from class so that lunchtimes run smoothly?

○ How are children promptly dismissed after eating?

○ Do children put their hands up so their plates or lunch boxes can be checked to ensure they have eaten enough?

○ Could your school afford to give teachers a free school meal if they sit and eat with the children?

○ Do your kitchen catering staff and midday supervisors have meetings and work together as a good team?

○ Is there time for dining hall supervisors to talk to a senior midday supervisor or teachers about their concerns regarding some children's eating problems.

○ Can you list three things that work well with your lunchtimes and dining halls?

○ Any other comments?

Trigger questions for teachers and teaching assistants not involved in the dining hall

- What do children complain most about to do with their dining halls and lunchtimes?

- Have you ever gone into the dining hall to see how your children are responding?

- Have the dining hall supervisors ever talked to you about children in your class not eating well or having any food problems?

- Have you, in any staff meetings, ever discussed the dining hall?

- Have you ever done any PSHE sessions on food, eating and the dining experience with your class?

- Do you discuss the menu options with the children before lunchtime?

- Do you ever show children pictures of the food, so they can choose their meal in advance?

- Are you aware of the research on children eating well and the link to their learning?

- Do you and parents/carers communicate with each other about eating at school?

- What is currently working well for your children and the dining hall and eating experience?

- Any other comments?

Trigger questions for catering staff and midday supervisors

○ Are you happy with the "look" of the dining hall?

○ Do you find the queues are too long?

○ Are you ever given a chance to be creative with food?

○ How do you find the time to make things extra special in the dining hall?

○ Are you aware of any themes of the term that you might be able to tie in with your own ideas?

○ Do you think the children speak respectfully to you – with please and thank you?

○ Are there Dining Hall Rules up in the dining hall?

○ Do you know what the Dining Hall Rules are off by heart?

○ Do you have meetings with your headteacher?

○ Are you invited to any school events?

○ What are noise levels like in the dining hall?

○ Does the noise in the dining hall stop you from hearing the children's voices?

○ What do you do when it gets too loud and noisy and when somebody needs to make an announcement?

○ Have you ever been encouraged to use the "hands up" approach to ask for quiet?

○ Do you think the children know their choices when they enter the hall and can they all make their choices easily (even the youngest)?

○ Are you given any rewards, incentives or stickers to hand out to the children?

○ How do you help slow eaters?

○ Do you have a slow eaters table that they can go on to finish their meal?

○ Do you have any system for how children should leave the dining hall – do they put their hand up for you to check their plate or lunch box?

○ Is there a lot of mess on and under the tables?

○ Do you have a system for scraping the plates and does it work well?

- Have you tried a "Golden Table of the Week" for children who keep the Dining Hall Rules?

- Do you ever have meetings with the other caterers, dining hall staff and yourself?

- Have you ever been invited to assemblies about the dining hall and how to make it happier?

- Do you have regular meetings with the catering team and senior managers together about the dining hall?

- How do you motivate your staff team?

- Do children ever complain to you about anything to do with the dining hall and food?

- Do you have a chance to speak to teachers about the children and their behaviour or eating?

- If you're ever worried about a child not eating who do you take this worry to?

- How do you find out about children's special dietary needs or issues – is it by talking to their teacher?

- What have you put in place recently that works well?

- Anything else about lunchtimes?

Trigger questions for pupils who have school meals

o   Do you like the school meals at your school?

o   Do you always get the choices that you want?

o   When you choose your meal in the morning, do you understand what the choices are?

o   Are you happy with where you sit for lunch?

o   Has a grown-up ever sat at your table to eat with you?

o   When you've finished your food do you put your hand up to wait for someone to check your plate?

o   If you are waiting for a midday supervisor does he/she come quickly?

o   Do you always finish your food?

o   Do you scrape your plate yourself, or does someone else do it for you?

o   Is there usually a lot of mess on or under your table?

o   Is the noise all right, or is it too loud in the dining hall?

o   How does it make you feel if noise in the dining hall is too loud?

o   Do you queue for too long to get your food?

o   Do you ever have stickers or anything for trying new food or for being quiet and tidy?

o   Have you ever been on a Golden Table of the Week?

o   If people are naughty at lunchtimes what happens?

o   Can you tell us anything else about lunchtimes?

Younger children can be asked the questions during a Circle Time and their responses written down by someone.

Trigger questions for pupils who have packed lunches

o   Do you like having a packed lunch at school?

o   Do you have some healthy food in your lunch box, like some fruit or vegetables?

o   Do you have treats in your lunch box, like sweets, chocolate or crisps?

o   Does a teacher or midday supervisor check what is in your lunch box?

o   Are you happy with where you sit for lunch?

o   Do grown-ups sometimes eat with you at your table?

o   When you've finished your food do you put your hand up to wait for someone to check your lunch box?

o   Do you put all your rubbish in the bin?

o   Is there usually a lot of mess on your table or under it?

o   Is the noise all right in the dining hall?

o   Do you ever have stickers, or anything else, for being quiet, polite or tidy?

o   Anything else about lunchtimes?

Trigger questions for parents

○ Do your children ever talk about the dining hall and the food they are offered?

○ Do you get menus sent home and do you have time to talk through the options with your child?

○ If your child is going through a funny stage about certain foods, have you ever written a letter, or talked to the teacher about it?

○ Are you aware that your child has salad choices?

○ Do your children know what "5 A DAY" means and the importance of fruit and vegetables?

○ If your child has a packed lunch, do you feel happy to know they have eaten their food or do you like them to bring wrappers back to show you what they have eaten?

○ Has your child ever talked about cookery, taster sessions or growing projects?

○ Has your child's teacher ever talked about your child's eating at school?

○ In the school brochure is there anything about "healthy eating" and/or what the school dining hall offers?

○ Is there anything else you would like to tell us about lunchtimes?

Ways forward

Clear a space in your diary for regular dining hall meetings.

➢ The best way forward is to create a whole school approach.

➢ Canvass all stakeholders for their views of the dining hall.

➢ Clear a space in your diary for regular dining hall meetings.

➢ Check in the school development plan if there's any way you can fit in staff meetings on the dining hall with the staff.

➢ Think about setting up a working party to help you keep a review of the whole school approach.

➢ Have a clear idea of where improvements are needed.

Chapter 4
Plan, do, review!

Nothing can change unless people feel that their views are included, that they are listened to and respected, and that decisions will be acted upon.

The simple mantra for change is: "PLAN, DO, REVIEW!"

Having looked at the trigger questions – maybe even had written responses or conversations with people, or just strong "gut" feelings that things need to change – is it possible for you to set up a series of meetings? Nothing can change unless people feel that their views are included, that they are listened to and respected, and that decisions will be acted upon.

The simple mantra for change is **"PLAN, DO, REVIEW!"**

The next few sections will help you identify what you most need to do. Some issues can be tackled quickly with the minimum of fuss, through quick discussions with key players and a quick assembly with the children where all key individuals are invited. Some issues, however, involve changing systems and that will involve meetings.

PLAN Get together and decide what you want to do, who's going to do it, by what date it will be done and don't leave this meeting without arranging the date of your next meeting, where you will review the success of the initiative.

Just everybody do what they said they would do!

DO Just everybody do what they said they would do!

REVIEW Did it work? Does it need adjusting? If it's a success put it on an "Our Success" board and elaborate it. So from now on, anything that's reviewed and seen as a success needs to go on this board to remind you to keep it going!

Ways forward

Review all the actions that have taken place and celebrate any successes.

➢ Look at all the information gathered so far.
➢ Create an action plan with important people, with the jobs everyone is going to do, who is doing it and the date of next meeting on it.
➢ Each person engaged with the plan needs to take action.
➢ Review all the actions that have taken place and celebrate any successes.

Chapter 5
The look and feel of the dining hall

Creating the right "look and feel" in your dining area is vital if you want the children to enjoy their lunchtime eating experience. There are lots of ways to make the environment more inviting, even on a limited budget.

"If you have an attractive dining space, with a happy atmosphere, people will want to eat there" (Judy Hargadon, School Food Trust).

Most school dining areas are used for other purposes throughout the day, so dining usually entails the use of removable furniture such as stackable tables and chairs. You may also be able to use additional indoor and outdoor spaces, such as a classroom, or an area of the playground. An awning over an outside area will ensure that it can be used in all weathers. Everywhere that is used must comply with health and safety regulations, so it is important to discuss these with the catering manager.

The appearance of the dining area can be made to be really inviting and welcoming.

Ideas for enhancing your dining hall

Below are a few ways I have thought of, but you may think of others!

➢ If your school is involved in a major building programme, look for any opportunities for the kitchens or dining area during this project.
➢ It may be worthwhile contacting local businesses to contribute paint or other items for redecoration and see if you can recruit volunteer decorators.

"If you have an attractive dining space, with a happy atmosphere, people will want to eat there" (Judy Hargadon, School Food Trust).

An awning over an outside area will ensure that it can be used in all weathers.

It may be worthwhile contacting local businesses to contribute paint or other items and see if you can recruit volunteer decorators.

Parents may be able to
volunteer useful skills
for your make-over or
donate items and reduce
the overall costs.

➢ Find out if there is a possibility of sponsorship from local organisations or of raising capital through fundraising events.

➢ Parents may be able to volunteer useful skills for your make-over or donate items and reduce the overall costs.

➢ You could incorporate a theme, having asked the children for ideas. Murals and good quality posters on walls can be very effective.

➢ Some schools create a gallery on one wall displaying items of art made by the children that can be refreshed at regular intervals. Local artists or businesses could be invited to provide a display or it may be a good place to proudly display art work from the school art club.

➢ Curtains or other items of soft furnishing add texture and colour to the area, and children may be more likely to treat their surroundings with respect if they are attractive and welcoming.

Waste food and bins
can be a real eyesore
so try and ensure left-
over food items are easy
to clear away but not
clearly visible to other
diners.

➢ Waste food and bins can be a real eyesore so try and make sure that leftover food items are easy to clear away, but not clearly visible to other diners (some schools put a bag on each table for children to put any waste or rubbish in).

➢ Rubbish trolleys can be a lot better than bins and easily moved around (see "Useful organisations" at the end of this book, p.93).

➢ It also helps if the room is at the right temperature and with good lighting – not too bright and glaring.

➢ Think about how your school allocates tables so that children can sit with their friends when appropriate.

Naming your dining hall

Some schools have
named their dining area,
as you would a café,
holding a competition to
think of the best name.

Some schools have named their dining area, as you would a café, (see Meadow Café photo on page 39), holding a competition amongst the children to think of the best name.

A panel of judges could be made up of children and staff and named or anonymous suggestions invited to be posted into a box. Making them anonymous means that the judges don't pick a name because it has been written by a friend.

Alternatively, the judges could make up a short list of five names and invite the whole school to vote for their favourite. Including the views of the children encourages a sense of ownership and care towards the dining area.

"We wanted to make it feel more like a cafe that children would experience in the real world" (Ian Read, headteacher, Watercliffe Meadow Community Primary School).

"We really didn't want our dining space to be like a typical school 'dining hall' and we wanted to make it feel more like a cafe that children would experience in the real world. We called it the Meadow Café and arranged the seating so that children could choose to sit in friendship groups. We did simple things like put flowers on the tables and put nice pictures of food on the walls. Just by doing these small things, it changed the experience for children, from just an eating space to a place for social interactions" (Ian Read, headteacher, Watercliffe Meadow Community Primary School, Sheffield).

Meadow Café, Watercliffe Meadow Community Primary School, Sheffield. This dining hall was named by the children and staff.

Creating dining zones

One zone for the youngest children could be cosier, quieter and with a décor that reflects their age ...

Some schools create different zones within their dining area to serve different purposes. For example, one zone for the youngest children could be cosier, quieter and with décor that reflects their age, or the zones could define different menus such as packed lunches and hot meals. If you buy any new furniture, do order different sizes to accommodate all ages.

Think carefully about where everything is placed.

Look at your dining hall carefully from the point of view of the children using it. I keep going into dining halls where the "scraping buckets" are the first thing that the children see when they are queuing up and it puts them off their food. Think carefully about where everything is placed.

Ways forward

➢ Think about getting the "right" look and feel for your dining hall so that it is welcoming and warm.

➢ Think carefully about where everything is placed.

➢ If, like most dining halls, the room has other uses, decide the best ways of multiple-usage of the room and how the furniture, layout and décor can help with all the purposes that the room serves.

➢ If any other areas could be used for dining consider opening them up for use.

Look for any possible opportunities for enhancing the look and feel of the room by using resourcefulness and creativity – often a working party is the best way forward.

➢ Look for any possible opportunities for enhancing the look and feel of the room by using resourcefulness and creativity – often a working party is the best way forward.

➢ Consider naming your dining hall to give it more character and helping with children's ownership of it.

➢ Think about having different zones to differentiate different functions of the dining room areas.

Chapter 6
Promoting positive behaviour

The behaviour of the children in the dining hall is an important aspect of creating a happy dining experience for both children and staff. Disruptive or inappropriate behaviour upsets everyone – staff and children alike.

Disruptive or inappropriate behaviour upsets everyone – staff and children alike.

Ofsted inspectors have been asked to "consider how lunchtime and the dining space contribute to good behaviour and the culture in the school" (Ofsted, 2013).

"Consider how lunch time and the dining space contribute to good behaviour and the culture in the school" (Ofsted, 2013).

Consider the following questions

➢ Do you or the senior management team have to frequently intervene to maintain acceptable behaviour?
➢ Have the supervisory staff been trained in how to motivate children with good rewards and incentives?
➢ If staff have had some training in managing children's behaviour positively and there are incentives to be used, what are the consequences if they break the rules?
➢ What behaviours are supervisory staff still worried about?
➢ Do children find the behaviour of some 'diners' intimidating or upsetting?
➢ Are behaviour incidents a frequent issue in the dining hall?

➢ Is there a set of "Dining Hall Rules" agreed by the staff and children and prominently displayed?

What behaviours are supervisory staff still worried about?

How to create calm

To encourage everyone to behave well in the dining hall, it is a good idea to first think through the situations that might lead to poor behaviour, for example, lengthy queues and waiting to enter the hall (see Chapter 7, pps.51-57), children waiting for too long to be released once they have finished eating – they will be eager to get out to play – or slow eaters (see pp.53, 72).

Think through the situations that may lead to poor behaviour

Creating a calm, quiet atmosphere within the dining area encourages calm, quiet behaviour in the children, which happens sooner when staff around them show considerate and kind behaviour towards the children. If the staff are intolerant and quick to criticise, prone to shouting or are grumpy, the children may respond by becoming irritable with each other or by acting out the same bad behaviour. Moods and bad humour are catching, but thankfully by the same token so are smiles, cheerfulness and warmth.

Are your dining hall behaviour expectations clear?

In your school you probably have drawn together some clear values that your whole school has agreed on. In my "Golden Model" we call these the "Golden Rules" (see p.47). These should be in every classroom, corridor, hall, playground and of course in the dining hall.

The Golden Rules are key values that enable adults and children to show respect for each other.

➢ Respect for physical safety is reflected in the rule "We are gentle"
➢ Respect for emotional safety is reflected in the rule "We are kind"
➢ Respect for the truth is reflected in the rule "We are honest"
➢ Respect for property is reflected in the rule "We look after things"
➢ Respect for each other is reflected in the rule "We listen"
➢ Respect for yourself is reflected in the rule "We work hard"

However midday supervisors, catering staff and children like to have their own voices and ideas. So pull them together and create a list called the "Dining Hall Routines". To make life simple we just call these the Dining Hall Rules and they can go up side by side with the school's Golden Rules.

   On p.47 you will see an example of the Dining Hall Rules that we put together for a school. You will notice that each one

We have included little cartoons on our posters as research has shown us that some children's minds are not stimulated just by the spoken and written word.

What incentives can you use to encourage children and adults to keep the Dining Hall Rules?

Children keep their full entitlement to Golden Time as long as they follow the Golden Rules.

can be linked back to the school Golden Rule. For example, "We keep our table clean" can be linked back to "We look after property", so the rules work well side by side. We have included little cartoons on our posters as research has shown us that some children's minds are not stimulated just by the spoken and written word. They need symbols, pictures or photographs as well: so some schools have now created their own images of children lining up calmly, using good table manners etc. Children need to know and understand the rules and Circle Times and assemblies are both good for introducing and reinforcing the "Rules". Also, putting your Dining Hall Rules poster in a proper frame will add gravitas!

So, your Dining Hall Rules are up and they have been discussed with the children and supervisory staff. What incentives can you use to encourage children and adults to keep them?

Positive behaviour encouragement through Golden Time

Golden Time is an incentives system that I developed many years ago and that was implemented by a large number of schools. Golden Time is a special activities time where children choose, once a week for Key Stage 2, or for a short while each day for Key Stage 1, to do a club or special activity that they really enjoy. The better the clubs and activities on offer, the better this works as an incentive. Children keep their full entitlement to Golden Time as long as they follow the Golden Rules. When they continue to break a Golden Rule after a warning, they quietly lose between one and five minutes of their Golden Time. Schools that use Golden Time as an incentive in the classroom can also use this as an incentive in the dining hall. The children are asked to keep the dining hall rules in the same way. If they break a rule they can be given a warning and if they continue to break a dining hall rule then a message can be sent to the teacher that they have lost five minutes of their weekly Golden Time (or 1 minute of their shorter daily Golden Time for Key Stage 1). This can be very motivating when it is done well. For more information about Golden Time see *Better Behaviour Through Golden Time* (Jenny Mosley, Helen Sonnet, LDA, 2005).

The Golden Table at Birchgrove Primary School, Swansea.

A Golden Table of the Week can inspire children to behave well

A Golden Table of the Week can be set up beautifully as a reward for children who have behaved well in the dining hall.

A Golden Table of the Week can be set up beautifully as a reward for children who have behaved well in the dining hall. You can use a golden table cloth, place mats, plastic golden goblets to drink from, flowers, napkins and anything to help children feel appreciated and feel that their good behaviour has been recognised. Midday supervisors choose different children each week to dine at this table. They can be selected for showing good table manners, being polite, trying new foods, talking quietly or for any other valid reason. Each child is allowed to invite a guest to eat with them on one day. The guest could be a child, parent/carer, grandparent, teacher or friend.

There is something wonderful about watching children and adults talking quietly and enjoying each other's company. Many children have "T.V. suppers" and they don't know the ritual of sitting down together to eat, chat, laugh and have good table manners at the same time. Because the table is so golden and sparkly, everyone's eyes are drawn to it. It gives children a picture of what they might one day like to create in their own home.

Dining Hall Targets of the Week and Golden Raffle Tickets

"Golden Raffle Tickets" are a way of raising behavioural expectations. Think about whatever is driving everyone mad about behaviour in the dining hall. Decide together which one behaviour everybody wants most to stop. If it's shouting, the target will be "We speak quietly." If it's messy tables it will be, "We keep our tables clean." If it's pushing and jostling, it's "We line up calmly."

Golden Raffle Tickets need to be introduced in assembly where the midday supervisors are invited along to explain how to use them.

The very best way to ask for quiet and to get everyone's attention is to use the "hands up" approach (p.56). This is where the midday supervisor raises his/her hand, and everyone else raises their hand too. With a great flourish he/she gets out the Golden Raffle Tickets and walks towards the children who have reached the target. Handing them a raffle ticket he/she says "Good choice, thank you for keeping your table so clean!" The child can take this back to their classroom, hand it to the teacher who can put a marble in the class "Jar of Good Choices." Children can also be given stickers for good choices. Stickers and posters in the dining hall are good reminders of the behaviours that are expected and noticed. Sometimes it is helpful if the sets of rules are sent home to parents.

I have been using these "targets" in several dining halls and a few midday supervisors complained that some children are just "putting it on." In other words they are exaggerating being polite to everyone because it's the target that is named and up in the

Some supervisors have a secret "Dining Hall Target of the Week" and when they spot the children doing it they quietly whisper their thanks and give the raffle ticket.

Some schools have mixed up their age groups in the dining hall so that older children can act as role models ... to younger children.

hall. So the supervisors decided to have a secret "Dining Hall Target of the Week" and when they spot the children doing it they quietly whisper their thanks and give the raffle ticket. The mystery element is now motivating more children!

Encouraging good table manners

A Golden Table of the Week helps to encourage good manners. Teachers can also help children with this by role-playing being in restaurants with the children in their classrooms – this can help with practicing laying the tables, using knives and forks, looking at menus and meal time conversations to help prepare children for using the dining facilities. Some schools have mixed up their age groups in the dining hall so that older children can act as role models, demonstrating good table manners and social skills to younger children. When staff eat their lunch alongside the children this acts as an extra opportunity to learn table manners, as well as helping to maintain good behaviour and build positive relationships through chatting and sharing a dining space.

 Dining hall posters to encourage positive behaviour!

What do we do if children break the Dining Hall Rules?

When children break the Dining Hall Rules, different schools will choose different consequences. Usually a member of staff will offer a quiet word to remind them of the rule and to let them know they are breaking it. After that, schools that have my Golden Model in place will often write out a small consequence notelet which can be handed to the senior midday supervisor and then passed to the teacher. This works alongside the Golden Time system and children will lose a small amount of Golden Time. (The opposite notelets can be given to children who are keeping the Dining Hall Rules as another incentive.) Photocopiable and printable notelets are included at the back of this book and on the accompanying CD-ROM. In schools that do not have the Golden Model in place then the consequence needs to tie in with the particular behaviour policy. In many schools the midday supervisors are very busy and may not have time to complete a notelet and something quick and easy may need to be found instead.

Photocopiable and printable notelets are included at the back of this book and on the accompanying CD-ROM.

The Golden Rules should sit alongside your Dining Hall Rules so that they both complement each other and provide a continuum of safe boundaries .

These colourful posters motivate children to keep the Dining Hall Rules

Thank you for cleaning your plate tidily.

Thank you for keeping the table clean.

Thank you for being polite to everyone.

Thank you for lining up calmly.

Thank you for walking carefully.

Thank you for speaking quietly.

Thank you for using good table manners.

Thank you for finishing your lunch today.

We have good manners in the dining hall when ...

We wait quietly in the line.
We say 'please' and 'thank you' to anyone helping us.
We keep our table and the space under it very clean.
We eat our food with our mouths closed.
We clean our plates tidily.

Designed by Jenny Mosley © 2014

Positive Press

Ways forward

The behaviour of the children in the dining hall is an important aspect of creating a happy dining experience.

Encourage good table manners by using the Golden Table of the Week.

➢ The behaviour of the children in the dining hall is an important aspect of creating a happy dining experience.

➢ Encourage everyone to behave well by thinking through the situations that might lead to poor behaviour.

➢ Creating a calm, quiet atmosphere within the dining area encourages calm, quiet behaviour in the children.

➢ Think whether your dining hall behaviour expectations are clear and your rules clearly displayed.

➢ Golden Table of the Week, Golden Raffle Tickets and Dining Hall Targets of the Week are ways of raising behavioural expectations.

➢ Encourage good table manners by using the Golden Table of the Week and teachers can role play this in class.

➢ If you need to use consequences when children break the Dining Hall Rules, which ones are appropriate to work alongside your systems?

Chapter 7
Do children have to queue for too long?

Why do we get queues?

A queue is a clue that some systems aren't working well!

A queue is a clue that some systems aren't working well. Queues may well happen if:

➢ Teachers let the children out late for lunch.
➢ Too many whole classes or year groups are released and go to the dining hall from class, or the playground, at the same time.
➢ Children are asked to queue up in the playground and have to wait for the whole class to line up before they can come in.
➢ Children are bunched up at the serving hatch not knowing what to choose.
➢ Children are waiting for items such as cutlery and water.

With a little forethought and careful planning queues can run much more smoothly.

Queuing to enter the dining hall can be a fraught experience for both children and adults, but with a little forethought and careful planning it can run much more smoothly. The first thing to do is to observe carefully to determine what hold ups there are:

Are there delays because children are unable to decide what to choose from the menu?

➢ Are there queues because too many children arrive at the dining hall at the same time?
➢ Are there delays because children are unable to decide what to choose from the menu?
➢ Are there other hold ups like searching for items like cutlery?

Once you know the cause or causes that contribute to long queues, you can develop action plans to deal with them.

Ideas on how to solve queuing problems

Often the first line of action is to stagger children's arrival at the dining hall more effectively.

Often the first line of action is to stagger children's arrival at the dining hall more effectively. This could mean changing the lunchtime for some children. In some schools, the last lesson of the morning is split in two for certain classes, so that the children dine earlier and resume their lesson whilst the rest of the school is still on their lunch break.

Another common cause for queues is when children take too long choosing their meal. One of more of the following may help:

➢ Display a menu board showing the day's options by the entrance to the dining hall so that children know what's on offer before they reach the serving area.

➢ Label the food to avoid children having to ask what each dish is.

➢ Print and display menus in classrooms or send them home for children to look at with their parents before arriving at the dining hall.

Post weekly or monthly menus on the school website for parents and pupils to access online.

➢ Post weekly or monthly menus on the school website for parents and pupils to access online.

➢ Teachers could take a few minutes each day to explain the choices to the children. This could be particularly helpful with younger children.

In schools with many languages it may be helpful to display photographs of the food.

➢ In schools with many languages, it could be helpful to display photographs of the food choices on the menu so that the children can see what's on offer.

➢ Children can make their choices before lunchtime and be given different coloured wrist bands to wear to indicate the veggie or meat meal of their choice. These can be seen at a glance by the supervisors and reduce serving time.

➢ Some dining halls can be arranged to have more than one serving area – providing several access points speeds up the process and reduces queues.

A mobile trolley with cold options can be positioned away from the main serving area.

➢ A mobile trolley with cold options can be positioned away from the main serving area, so that the queue only contains children who want hot meals.

➢ Look at the way the meals are served and utensils dispensed to see if this process could be speeded up.

Dining Hall Helpers may be able to help children move more smoothly through the "system".

➢ "Dining Hall Helpers" (see Chapter 9) may be able to help children move more smoothly through the "system" by helping at various decision or action points.

➢ Does your school use "airline trays" for main meals and desserts or separate plates and bowls? The former does reduce serving time, although some schools are reverting to using plates to improve the aesthetics.

➢ Have cutlery sets available away from serving areas to allow children to move away more quickly.

➢ Ensure water can be accessed by children themselves – I have been to schools where water is provided in such large pitchers only the adults can pour the water. Children then have to wait for an available adult and will often wander off without water.

Children may be holding up movement within the queue as they look for a place to sit.

Children may be holding up movement within the queue once they have their food as they look for a place to sit. If you have set sittings, each child could have a designated seat that they always go to. On the other hand some children don't like "set" seats at all so some schools let them sit anywhere! If children enter the dining hall on a rolling system, there could be an area away from the queue for children to move to when looking for a place to sit. Alternatively, an adult supervisor can note empty seats and direct children to them once they have their meal.

Perhaps having a cash-based payment system in your dining hall is holding up the queue? Canteen-style dining halls, where pupils pay for their food, is more common in post-primary education, but it is a fact that paying for food at a "checkout" can worsen queues or create bottle-necks. So it is useful to quickly mention here how cashless systems, such as contactless smart cards that parents/children top up, can speed up the queuing process. Children use these cards at the "point of transaction", rather than rummaging for their dinner money. Another benefit of this payment method is that it gives those who are entitled to universal free school meals a discreet way of receiving their food.

It may be a good idea to have a designated table for slow eaters so that they do not feel under pressure.

Slow eating children can also affect the queuing in the dining hall and it may be a good idea to have a separate designated table for them or allow slow eaters in the dining hall first (see p.72 for more on slow eaters).

Solving a queuing problem

In one school I visited I saw the midday supervisor in the playground waiting too long trying to get the whole class into a line, which created an unnecessary delay for the kitchen staff while waiting for them to come in. We therefore created a system where, when the first eight children had arrived in the line they could go in together, and then the next eight and so on, which helped to keep food service going even if the whole class was not quite ready to go in at once.

Ways forward

➢ Try to work out why the queues are happening – queues usually form because of the timings of classes coming into the hall – and then take steps to resolve the issues.
➢ Ensure that children know their food choices before they get to the dining hall.
➢ Ask teachers to send children promptly to their lunch.
➢ Stagger lunch sittings.
➢ Dining Hall Helpers may help with the queuing process.
➢ Post weekly, monthly or termly menus on the school website for parents and pupils to access online or include the information in regular newsletters to parents.

Queues usually form because of the timings of classes coming into the hall.

Chapter 8
Is your dining hall too noisy?

What is too noisy?

Noisy environments can be very stressful for some children – and for many adults. If your midday supervisors are having to shout to make themselves heard above the chatter, then the noise levels are too high.

Some situations always bring on an increase in volume. For example, if children are queuing for too long, waiting for permission to leave the dining area once they have eaten, or if behaviour guidelines are not clear or easy to follow, then the volume will go up. An acceptable level of noise is easier to maintain if staff can reduce the noise before it is necessary to shout.

Children become confused if on one day staff demand silence and the following day a different set of staff allow loud chatter and laughter, so it is best to aim for a consistent level or volume of noise.

Ideas for quietening the hall

Some schools like to play background music to encourage quieter conversations or invite musicians – either pupils from within the school or visitors – to enhance the dining experience and encourage the children to listen, and also to be quiet and eat. Sometimes though, background music can just create more noise as children try to talk over it. Mind you, when I have been in dining halls where children are playing music on the stage, most children do quieten down to listen as they are fascinated by other children's talents.

If your midday supervisors have to shout ... then the noise levels are too high.

Sometimes though, background music can just create more noise as children try to talk over it.

The brilliant traffic light system

In one school I worked in, children said "why don't we have a flag going up the side of the wall next to a painted stripe going from green, to orange to red?"

In one school I worked in, children came up with a lovely idea – in fact children always have brilliant ideas to solve problems – they said "why don't we have a flag going up the side of the wall next to a painted stripe going from green, to orange to red?". The flag is normally on green which means the noise is ok. But when the flag is pulled up by the midday supervisor to orange, this indicates that noise levels are getting too loud and if it reaches red we all know that noise levels are too high. So a midday supervisor may well want to raise her hand (see below) and announce that they have just moved into the orange danger zone. Children don't like to reach the red zone because at the top of it is a ledge with a one minute sand timer on it and everyone has to have to have a one minute silence using the sand timer, which the midday supervisor will turn over and time.

Getting everyone's attention – the hands up approach

The hands up approach works, but only if the whole school practices the method in assemblies and classrooms.

One great way of reminding children that the noise level is creeping up is called the "hands up" approach. In a school I was working in the dining hall staff had taken to using a whistle, it was quite ear-splitting and it added to the noise, which only died down for a second while they shouted the instructions to the children, then the noise would come back again. We decided to work on a whole school approach to getting silence which involved all the lunchtime, dining and catering supervisors. The hands up approach works, but only if the whole school practices the method in assemblies and classrooms. Then the senior managers need to come into the dining hall and model it by letting the dining hall staff put their hand up first and then by following suit. The adult should not speak with their hand up.

For this system, the adult puts their hand up. Any other adults in the dining hall put their hands up too and walk swiftly to any children who are chatting, tap them on the shoulder and point to the adult who has their hand up, but they mustn't talk, just point. The children know that if they spot an adult with their hand up they must stop chatting and tap any other chatting children on the shoulder and point to that adult. The adult then waits until everyone is quiet and with their hand up and looking at them, then puts their hand down and speaks to the crowd. Sometimes their hand is up because they have a Golden Raffle Ticket in it and they are thrilled with a good behavioural choice!

Ways forward

➤ Work out if your dining hall is too noisy. If staff are having to shout and it is difficult to get everyone's attention, chances are it is too noisy.

➤ Try to avoid situations that always bring on an increase in volume, such as long queues, waiting for staff, or when behaviour guidelines are not clear.

➤ Have an indicator for noise levels so that children can see when noise levels are getting too high.

➤ Some schools use a traffic light system to control noise levels: displaying green at the bottom for normal noise levels; orange above, for when it is getting too loud and red at the top, to let everyone know it is too noisy.

➤ An effective way of reminding children when the noise level begins to creep up is called the hands up approach.

Try to avoid situations that always bring on an increase in volume, such as long queues, waiting for staff, or when behaviour guidelines are not clear.

Chapter 9
Dining Hall Helpers

Dining Hall Helpers and their roles

Some schools ask older pupils if they would like to help in the dining hall.

Children can pick up an application form and apply for the role they would most like to work in.

Some schools ask older pupils if they would like to help in the dining hall and these would be called Dining Hall Helpers. To increase the status of their position, it is a good idea to take a fairly formal approach to recruitment. Schools often create a job description, which is posted up, listing the tasks involved in the role. Children can pick up an application form and apply for the role or prospective helpers are invited to apply for a position as a Dining Hall Helper. Application forms are signed by parents/carers and teachers. In some schools children are interviewed too. Dining Hall Helper tasks can be decided by lunchtime staff and how your dining hall is organised. Here are some ideas:

➤ Preparing the tables. This might include laying a table with a cloth, cutlery, glasses and water.
➤ Helping diners, especially younger children with their meal choices.
➤ Helping to seat diners, especially younger children, and helping to cut up their food or showing them how to do it.
➤ Serving salad or other cold choices (Health and Hygiene rules apply).
➤ Refilling water jugs throughout the meal times.
➤ Walking around the dining hall and asking diners to pick up dropped items and clear away rubbish before they leave the dining hall.
➤ Helping diners, especially younger children, to clear away their cutlery.
➤ Being available to run errands and carry out jobs for lunchtime staff.
➤ Don't forget to ask the caterers too what job they would like help with.
➤ Having special Dining Hall Helper aprons/tabards and hats

would make the Dining Hall Helpers clearly visable in the dining hall.

Incentives for Dining Hall Helpers

Dining Hall Helpers are often offered something in return for carrying out their tasks. This might be free meals or other privileges and parents/carers will need to be kept informed. In many schools, teachers claim that just having the privilege of the role and wearing a Dining Hall Helper uniform – such as an apron and hat/hairnet, like the catering staff – boosts a child's self-esteem and they don't need any extra incentive. Whatever your school decides to offer, it should confer status to the student helpers so that other children see the role as important.

To enable as many children as possible to experience the role of helper, the duration of their work experience can be limited to a half term. A "Certificate of Appreciation" signed by the caterers and lunchtime staff should be awarded once the Dining Hall Helpers have finished their duty period. You can also use the "award" as an incentive to help a child towards being responsible in a school setting. This could be especially important for those children with low self-esteem or who have social and emotional difficulties.

It is a good idea to get a senior school manager to meet with the Dining Hall Helpers for just five minutes a week to ask them how their job is going.

Training Dining Hall Helpers

Dining Hall Helpers need to be trained for the role that they will be playing and be invited to appropriate meetings. Incentives for them include, being thanked in assembly, going to meetings and having a "thank you" certificate.

Do see in the Case Studies section, Kew Riverside Primary School – they have written up about their fantastic "Lunchtime Helpers"!

A "Certificate of Appreciation" ... should be awarded once the Dining Hall Helpers have finished their duty period.

Dining Hall Helpers need to be trained for the role that they will be playing and be invited to appropriate meetings.

Ways forward

➢ Some schools ask older pupils if they would like to be a Dining Hall Helper in the dining hall.

➢ Pupils can apply for a Dining Hall Helper position by completing an application form and sometimes having an interview with staff.

➢ Uniforms will make Dining Hall Helpers clearly visible in the dining hall.

➢ Dining Hall Helpers will benefit from training so that they know what to do and they can be invited to appropriate meetings.

➢ Think about the incentives for Dining Hall Helpers which could include a "thank you" in the form of an acknowledgment in front of the school, a certificate or a complimentary lunch.

Unifoms can make Dining Hall Helpers clearly visible in the dining hall.

Chapter 10
Promoting healthy eating

At the beginning of this book we said we were not able to address food and menus here. However, we are well placed to make a few general suggestions and signpost where to go for further information.

Linking eating and learning

Encouraging healthy eating is an important aspect of the dining hall, especially with the rise in childhood obesity and other weight-related conditions that threaten the future wellbeing of some pupils.

In spring 2015, Ofsted announced an intention to place greater importance on healthy eating when carrying out inspections.

In spring 2015, Ofsted announced an intention to place greater importance on healthy eating when carrying out inspections. In September 2015 the "Common Inspection Framework" will include a judgement on "personal development, behaviour and welfare". Inspectors will look for a culture and ethos of excercise and healthy eating throughout their entire inspection visit; placing greater emphasis on schools to work on supporting pupils to gain knowledge of keeping themselves healthy through excercise and healthy eating.

Encouraging healthy eating is not just important for overall health, as it increasingly being shown that eating nutritious food can help with academic results and attendance.

Encouraging healthy eating is not just important for overall health, it increasingly being shown that eating nutritious food can help with academic results, behaviour and attendance. As we mentioned earlier (see p.22), research carried out for Jamie Oliver's "Feed Me Better" campaign in Greenwich, showed that "English and Science test results rose significantly among 11-year olds and absenteeism owing to sickness has fell by 14%" (Belot and James, 2009).

Eating, nutrition and Personal, Social, Health and Economic Education (PSHE) programmes

The Government's PSHE education review in March 2013 stated that PSHE would remain non-statutory and that no new programmes of study would be published. However, in the "National Curriculum Framework" the DfE states that "All schools should make provision for personal, social, health and economic education (PSHE), drawing on good practice" (DfE, 2013).

The existing PSHE programme of study for key stages 1 to 4 is based on three themes:

1. Health and Wellbeing
2. Relationships
3. Living in the Wider World.

So, it is clear to see that healthy eating and a healthy attitude towards food is a part of this programme. The PSHE Association (see Useful Organisations p.94) provides support and resources for PSHE practitioners.

With PSHE, schools find they can make great cross-curricular links involving learning about food production, food tasting, cookery, food preferred by people of different cultures and plant growing projects.

Taster sessions

Taster sessions in the classroom and dining hall are a good idea and provide the children with an opportunity to try out small portions of a range of foods. If tasting sessions are carried out in the classroom children will have longer to pluck up the courage to taste something different. The fact that they can see other children eating and enjoying different food will also encourage them to be brave. If you make this a topic, the children can discuss flavours, health values and preferences.

"All schools should make provision for personal, social, health and economic education (PSHE), drawing on good practice" (DfE, 2013).

If tasting sessions are carried out, children will have longer to pluck up the courage to taste something different.

Is banning unhealthy foods a good idea?

Some schools promote healthy eating by banning unhealthy options. So, for example, they might not allow fizzy drinks or chocolate bars in lunch boxes or as snacks, and sometimes crisps may only be brought to school on a Friday. Some schools have a tuck shop that stocks healthy and nutritious snacks.

It is important to find out children's opinions on the food that they are offered.

It is important to find out children's opinions on the food that they are offered. This will highlight the foods that they enjoy and make sure that they are not being continually offered choices that they do not like. It may also provide ideas for new ranges to be included in the menu.

Some ways to raise the profile of healthy eating within school

Below are some examples of achievable ways of promoting healthy eating.

Hold a food festival each year and invite parents.

Hold a food festival each year and invite parents. Photographs of different meals can be displayed and parents can sample some of the dishes.

Run a parent's competition to find a new dish for the school offering a prize and naming the dish after the winner e.g. Mr Carter's Pasta Surprise.

Encourage children to grow their own food produce.

Encourage children to grow and cook their own food produce by promoting growing and cooking projects. A gardening club is a good way of activating the children's interest and providing them with important information about where vegetables come from and how to prepare and cook them. In 2014 Jamie Oliver's "Kitchen Garden Project" was launched for UK primary schools to meet the new compulsory food education curriculum in England. Schools joining the project can access recipes, lesson plans, posters, fact sheets and gardening resources.

A cookery club can help children to want to try out new healthy dishes.

A cookery club will get children involved in the preparation and cooking of food so that they understand exactly what a dish contains and then they are more likely to have a taste or to try out new dishes.

Other opportunities to promote healthy eating may be through breakfast or after school clubs. Breakfast clubs are great for ensuring that children have a good, healthy breakfast to see them through the morning.

As an example of a school promoting healthy eating, do see our case study from Smith's Wood Primary Academy – it's fantastic!

Ways forward

➢ Encouraging healthy eating is an important aspect of the dining hall, especially with the rise in childhood weight-related conditions.

➢ The presentation of food plays an important role in attracting children and should look fresh and delicious.

➢ Taster sessions are a good idea and provide the children with new opportunities to taste different foods.

➢ Some schools promote healthy eating by banning unhealthy options.

➢ It is important to ask the children's opinions on the food that they are offered which will highlight the food that they enjoy.

➢ Breakfast clubs are great for ensuring that children have a good, healthy breakfast to see them through the morning.

➢ There are many ways to raise the profile of healthy eating within a school and sometimes thinking creatively helps here!

Breakfast clubs are great for ensuring that children have a good, healthy breakfast to see them through the morning.

The presentation of food plays an important role in attracting children and should look fresh and delicious.

There are many ways to raise the profile of healthy eating within a school and sometimes thinking creatively helps here!

Chapter 11
Signposting to other people, organisations and initiatives

The following people and organisations are some suggestions of who to turn to for further advice and inspiration on healthy nutrition and more – for their, and other, websites see page 94.

- ➢ Jeanette Orrey and the Food for Life Partnership
- ➢ Jamie Oliver
- ➢ Food Dudes
- ➢ The School Food Plan
- ➢ Healthy Schools Initiatives

Jeanette Orrey and the Food for Life Partnership

Jeanette Orrey, MBE, is a leading children's food campaigner and former school catering manager. Jeanette has been an inspiration for Jamie Oliver's campaign to improve school meals and is the School Meals Policy Advisor at the Soil Association. As an author, her first book *The Dinner Lady: Change The Way Your Children Eat Forever* (Bantam, 2005) is especially well known.

"My vision is that every child has a right to good wholesome school food and that food poverty will be a thing of the past" (Jeanette Orrey, MBE).

"My vision is that every child has a right to good wholesome school food and that food poverty will be a thing of the past" (Jeanette Orrey, MBE).

Jeanette is also co-founder of the Food for Life Partnership, a programme all about "transforming food culture – making healthy, tasty and nutritious meals the norm for all to enjoy, reconnecting people with where food comes from, teaching them how it's grown and cooked and understanding the importance of well-sourced ingredients".

Jamie Oliver

Jamie Oliver launched a major, and original campaign, to bring the issue of school food and children's nutrition into the limelight in 2005, with a television series, media articles and a website. He has worked tirelessly since then championing children's health and school nutrition.

"We can't underestimate the importance of investing in our children's health and productivity at school" (Jamie Oliver).

"We can't underestimate the importance of investing in our children's health and productivity at school. Getting cooking on the curriculum until the age of 14 and encouraging kids to eat school food are big steps, and we really need to get behind school cooks and headteachers to improve school food" (Jamie Oliver).

In 2010 Jamie was awarded the prestigious TED Prize for creating a strong, sustainable movement to educate every child about food, inspire families to cook again and empower people everywhere to fight obesity.

The Jamie Oliver Food Foundation is a charity "that aims to inspire people to reconnect with food. It's all about raising awareness and individual responsibility, resuscitating dying food culture around the world and, ultimately, keeping cooking skills alive".

Food Dudes

Devised by a team of leading academics and underpinned by peer-reviewed research evidence, the award winning Food Dudes healthy eating programme combines behavioural change interventions with fun activities to increase fruit and vegetable consumption in children. The Food Dudes programme is delivered through nursery, primary and special schools, and has been implemented with over 700,000 children and achieves consistently impressive results.

Their research revealed that:

➢ It is common for children to eat 100% more fruit and vegetables per day by end of the programme

- ➢ Results are sustained in the long-term, with Food Dudes proven to have a positive impact on food choices more than 2.5 years after participation
- ➢ Consumption of sweet and fatty (junk) foods also typically decreases by between 20% and 50%
- ➢ Results transfer from school to home, with parents reporting increased fruit and vegetable consumption
- ➢ Results are unaffected by the socio-economic status and ethnicity of participants
- ➢ Food Dudes actually works best with the fussiest of eaters

Remarkably, many other programmes that run to combat obesity provide no independent evidence in support of their effectiveness. One of the distinguishing features of the Food Dudes approach is that it is firmly grounded in scientific evidence, most of which is from controlled experimentation, as well as being replicable.

One of the distinguishing features of the Food Dudes approach is that it is firmly grounded in scientific evidence.

The Food Dudes programme is delivered by leading academics, scientists and specialists from psychology, health and education backgrounds.

The School Food Plan

Many parents mistakenly imagine that a packed lunch is the healthiest option. In fact, it is far easier to get the necessary nutrients into a cooked meal – even one of mediocre quality. Only 1% of packed lunches meet the nutritional standards that currently apply to school food" (Dimbleby and Vincent, 2013).

"Only 1% of packed lunches meet the nutritional standards that currently apply to school food" (Dimbleby and Vincent, 2013).

The School Food Plan is an agreed plan that has the support of the Secretary of State for Education and other relevant organisations to support headteachers to improve food in their schools. The plan recognises that since Jamie Oliver alerted Britain about the state of school food nutrition in 2005, measurable improvements have been made. This plan was created to build upon these findings and to educate children about growing, cooking and eating proper food. It is also about improving the academic performance of our children and the health of our nation.

Healthy Schools Initiatives

"Healthy schools" or "Health-promoting Schools" approaches help to translate the whole school approach into practice and enhance the health and educational outcomes of their pupils

"Healthy schools" or "Health-promoting Schools" approaches help to translate whole school approach into practice and enhance the health and educational outcomes of their pupils.

For schools that follow a local Healthy Schools programme, most of these programmes involve a whole school audit (usually online) to help schools identify and implement effective school based strategies to address current health priorities. Schools are often supported to implement and monitor the impact of their health related interventions for pupils. For example, the Wiltshire Healthy Schools programme has a bronze level involving an online audit of provision, while silver level asks schools to submit evidence to show how they are implementing further good practice and making measurable improvements to the health and wellbeing of their pupils. The Gold level offers a unique opportunity for schools to showcase their sustained commitment to the health and wellbeing of their pupils.

Many local authorities now support schools through their own local Healthy Schools programme.

By using a whole school approach, schools can enhance the health and educational outcomes of their pupils. Many schools achieved "National Healthy Schools" status, a programme which helped schools translate this approach into practice. Many local authorities now support schools through their own local Healthy Schools programme. Schools can find out details of their current local Healthy Schools programme from their local authority School Improvement or Public Health officers.

Chapter 12
Further considerations

With large numbers of staff and children, there will always be other issues to consider in the dining hall.

The following six items are some that we are NOT able to cover in this book, but that are very important to your overall dining systems and will require specialist support and policies.

➢ Eating disorders
➢ Food phobias
➢ Food allergies and intolerances
➢ Bullying around food issues
➢ Children who are overweight
➢ Pupils with special educational needs (SEN)

It is vital that you balance an understanding of children's individual needs with ensuring they do not feel alienated from other children and ensure that teachers, midday supervisors and parents or carers are kept in regular dialogue as well.

The following items are also very deserving of consideration and we have written a short piece about each below

Cultural preferences

Cultural preferences relating to food and eating should also be considered, so that nobody feels isolated from the dining experience enjoyed by others. Asking children and parents/carers for their views is helpful in making the dining hall really inclusive – working with parents/carers is really important here and this is sometimes done through the Healthy Schools Awards projects. We cannot stress how important it is to keep the channels of communication open with parents/carers.

It is vital that you balance an understanding of children's individual needs with ensuring they do not feel alienated from other children.

Cultural preferences relating to food and eating should also be considered.

Some schools have different coloured trays for different types of diet for instance, one colour for Asian vegetarian, one for British vegetarian, one for meat options etc.

Slow eaters

Some children like to eat their lunch at a very slow pace – we are told that this can be very good for digestion. If you have a group of slow eating children, are they eating slowly because they're frightened of going outside or eating slowly because they don't like the food? Maybe they just naturally eat slowly? Slow eaters scattered throughout the dining hall can slow up the dining hall systems and slow down queues. One idea is to let the slow eaters into the dining hall first, or it may be a good idea to have a designated table for slow eaters, so that they do not feel under pressure to eat as quickly as other children on their table. This allows the other tables to be cleaned down ready for the next sitting or as part of the post-lunch tidy up. If they are not being constantly chivvied to "hurry up" by pupils and staff, their dining experience will be more relaxed and enjoyable. We need to notice who is on this table so we can talk about their individual needs.

It may be a good idea to have a designated table for slow eaters so that they do not feel under pressure to eat as quickly as other children on their table.

Keeping packed lunches healthy

Packed lunches can be a tricky area, for example, how do you ensure lunch boxes are balanced and healthy – do children with packed lunches have a separate eating area or are they allowed to sit with their friends who eat a cooked lunch? These are important considerations and some schools may operate a packed lunch policy and this sets out the sorts of foods that the school encourages children to have in their lunch boxes and seating set ups. However, packed lunches can be a sensitive area as some parents/carers may not like being told what they can put in their children's lunch boxes and so communication with parents/carers is key. Schools that have gone for the Healthy Schools Award should already be in regular contact with parents/carers about what makes a nutritious and enjoyable packed lunch. The Children's Food Trust is a good place to start if you want more information on packed lunches and they offer downloadable packed lunch templates.

Schools that have gone for the Healthy Schools Award should already be in regular contact with parents about what makes a nutritious and enjoyable packed lunch.

Communicating with each other about children's food habits, needs and problems

Midday supervisors, lunchtime supervisors, and catering staff are very rushed. They do their best to try and notice children having a problem with their food and often children need to put their hand up for a supervisor to check their lunch box or tray before they leave the dining hall.

But let's be realistic. Some children sneak away so the supervisor does not notice that they haven't eaten all their food. Some children throw any food they don't want to eat on the floor. Sometimes when I'm in a playground I find lunch boxes emptied behind trees or plants. The real issue is how we let each other know. Are parents/carers encouraged to come in and talk about food problems? Are teachers encouraged to talk to the midday supervisors? What system is in operation in your school? Some schools have senior midday supervisors – to whom all other supervisors go to tell their worries or what they have noticed. One of the senior supervisor's tasks is to take the information about individual children back to the teachers so that the teachers can talk to the parents/carers. However, everyone is in a rush and if it's not been flagged up in regular meetings then it's one of the key weaknesses in your system.

Schools need to communicate with parents/carers about packed lunch and school meal policies and share any concerns they have about individuals. Catering staff need to be heard too because they are right on the front line of children being very picky eaters and they need advice as to whether they are allowed to give them smaller portions in such cases. I have talked to catering managers who are convinced they have to give everyone the same sized portion as it is a legal requirement. But the large amount of food on their tray sometimes puts the child off.

Circle Time and dining halls

Circle Times can be great for canvassing children's opinions about dining halls and can also be used to discuss ideas like reducing noise and queues. New ideas can be talked through and

Some children sneak away so the supervisor does not notice that they haven't eaten all their food

One of the senior supervisor's tasks is to take the information about individual children back to the teachers.

Catering staff need to be heard too because they are right on the front line of children being very picky eaters.

Circle Times can be great for canvassing children's opinions about dining halls.

children love to come up with their own solutions! Reinforcing the Dining Hall Rules and getting children excited about food and growing projects are also better in a circle. For more information about Circle Times, for Circle Time resources and training go to www.circle-time.co.uk.

Making the dining hall fun and educational at the same time!

I have met some truly amazing unit catering managers, midday supervisors and catering assistants in schools who make the whole dining experience fabulous and fun in many different ways.

I have met some truly amazing unit catering managers, midday supervisors and catering assistants in schools who make the whole dining experience fabulous and fun in many different ways. Here are some that I have heard about or actually seen in action:

➢ Curriculum themed lunchtimes – geographical, historical, science etc.
➢ Dressing up for lunch days – the catering staff dress up based on theme the pupils have voted for or the pupils can dress up if feasible/practical.
➢ International menu days – celebrating different cultures and countries.
➢ Food allergy awareness days – a gluten free day, to show what it is like to be a Coeliac for example.
➢ Favourite food days – pupils could vote for their favourite meals.
➢ Lunchtime lottery – children who keep the dining hall rules get a lottery ticket and then the tickets are pulled out of a hat at the end of the week and the winner wins a prize or they win a prize for the class!
➢ Competitions.
➢ Decorating the service area.
➢ Reward stickers and prizes!

Posters and displays can really be your friend when cultivating new initiatives and promoting new ideas.

… the list could go on and on!

Posters and stickers

Posters and displays can really be your friend when cultivating new initiatives and promoting new ideas. Healthy eating, pictures of everyday food, pictures of food from different cultures, information about food allergies, can all be displayed beautifully in the dining hall. We always advocate that your school's Golden Rules and Dining Hall Rules are clearly displayed where everyone can see them.

Stickers are a great way of reinforcing positive behaviour in the dining hall.

Stickers are a great way of reinforcing positive behaviour in the dining hall, such as tasting new foods, and anything positive connected with lunchtimes and the dining hall.

Ways forward

➢ Cultural preferences – people with different cultures may need different considerations regarding food and customs.
➢ Slow eaters – these pupils need consideration so that they aren't unnecessarily rushed.
➢ Packed lunches – are packed lunches healthy and can pupils bringing them sit with friends who are having school lunches?..
➢ Allergies and food intolerances – it is important to find out which pupils have which intolerances and to create policies to protect and integrate those pupils.
➢ Food and anti-bullying – it is as well to remember that weight and food-related issues can make children stand out and become victims of bullying and staff should be trained to be aware of this and know how to act.
➢ Staff should be able to talk to other staff and parents to ensure children are happy and eating well.
➢ It is great to make the dining hall fun and educational at the same time.
➢ Posters and stickers can help to spread ideas, give praise and remind everyone of rules and various initiatives.

Its great to make the dining hall fun and educational at the same time.

Chapter 13
Case Studies

I have truly seen lunchtimes at their very best and at their very "ripe for radical improvement"! Below are some very different tales.

CASE STUDY 1

A true lunchtime experience that made me want to cry!

I recently visited an ordinary dining hall in a school that had only recently been awarded the Ofsted "Outstanding". It has about 500 children and at least 40 more children are now receiving hot school meals. I don't know what has tipped the balance from Outstanding to "Chaotic" – maybe the Ofsted inspectors failed on their last visit to line up with their airline tray to eat with the children! I do it every time I visit a school in order to get to the heart of what is and isn't working in a school.

The day I was in teachers were obviously releasing the children late to come into lunch. You could see the irritation on the midday supervisors' faces. I wondered how many times this has happened to the dining hall staff.

I watched the TAs see the young children into the dining hall door and then disappear. They did not see them right into the line for the hatch – so the young children were running across the hall to get to the line.

One child new to hot dinners was crying and one midday supervisor (there were only two in the hall) spent ages trying to get him to eat. He was becoming more distressed the more she reasoned with him. Near me a child was also crying, but I just focussed on the children around him, praising them for trying new food and giving them a sticker. Quietly through the tears he watched what went on and tentatively tried a bit of food. Quietly I gave him a sticker and a shy smile appeared.

The first thing the children saw on their way to the hatch was the leftovers from the previous children being scraped into the bins. The children weren't doing this themselves, a midday supervisor was rushing backwards and forwards, and in the queue to get their plates scraped the children were losing interest and slowly their plates tipped towards the floor, so there was a nasty sludgy mess around the bins. Because the "scraping-food" midday supervisor was so busy she wasn't able to notice which children were leaving all their food. This was important, as there was no other system in the dining hall for spotting which children weren't eating properly and whose names needed to go to their parent/carer via their teacher.

As I was eating and chatting to the children, the two queues for the hatch got longer and longer as they brought whole classes in at a time! The children waited around in this line getting bored. Very soon the "class clowns" took the opportunity to hype up their excited behaviour or the other children just wound somebody else up. The noise became deafening and the children got so distracted they didn't notice it was their turn to move to the hatch, so the catering staff kept having to call them to queue up.

Suddenly from nowhere a whistle shrieked – the "running around" midday supervisor had had enough and this was the way she got silence. Unfortunately she shrieked after the whistle. There was a shocked silence for a very few seconds and the noise started to build up again very quickly.

Children at the hatch took ages to choose their food. "Yes", said the catering staff "we do give them menus – look they're up there". I looked up and the menus were there in small writing. Small children would have to crane their necks and wouldn't be able to read the menus anyway. There was no concept of having photographs of the meals earlier in the queue for them to study. Also, I later found out that the teachers never did any prior work in the classroom on what lunchtime food choices there were and there was never any discussion with the children about how they were faring in the dining hall. In fact the children I talked to said they never had circle time or just had it occasionally when there had been a fight in the playground.

Next to the scraping-food midday supervisor there was a table with big jugs full up with water – too heavy for any children to take to their own table. No older children ever had the system of looking after younger children – so none of the jugs ever got to the tables. I only saw a handful of children in the whole hall drink any water.

When eating with the children they told me they hated the noise; they hated having to go out to play with messy hands (they would like napkins or sinks outside) and they didn't like it that some children threw food under the table, as it put them off eating. I asked them as they weren't drinking water in the hall where did they get their water – they said they had a water fountain outside, but however you angled your head you could only get a few mouthfuls before someone pushed you in the back out of the way. "And by the way Miss, if you're a new supply teacher please tell someone the toilets are really smelly and full of water and we don't like going in there either".

When they had finished their food there was no system for putting up their hands for the midday supervisors to check their tray to see if they could go. Rather than queue up for a midday supervisor to scrape their plates, a handful of them just left their tray on the table and scarpered.

A lunchtime experience that made me want to sing and dance!

Smith's Wood Primary Academy, Solihull

Occasionally in my work in schools I come across truly golden practice and a short time ago I stumbled across a dining hall pot of gold! At Smith's Wood Primary Academy the food is as colourful and beautifully presented as the dining hall itself! The dining hall staff are most positive and are often seen dressing up for themed events. The unit catering manager is amazing – the last time I met her she was encouraging the children to learn about the rainforest. So she wrote the word 'Rainforest" using fruit and vegetables and decorated the plate with a rainforest collage.

The school has been piloting a "Food Dudes" approach to encouraging healthy eating and also using taster sessions and initiatives, such as the hands up approach to getting quiet in the hall. Children are also shown the choices of food on a white board in the mornings to reduce queuing times at lunch time. This school is so proactive – thank you to the Headteacher John Talbot and Unit Catering Manager Julia Underwood, who have written accounts for the book. Do see the colourful photographs at the end of this case study!

Headteacher, John Talbot

"Lunchtimes are about an hour of the school day. The lessons may have ended but the learning continues. By working closely with the kitchen, themed lunchtimes can directly enhance what is going on in the classroom. More than this, themed sessions can be fun and help develop a positive atmosphere at lunchtimes. The teaching of table manners and eating etiquette are also part of the 'hidden curriculum' that goes on at lunchtime. Also, as a large school with high levels of deprivation and Universal Free School Meals now in place, we have to be well organised and efficient to ensure that lunchtimes do not stretch into lesson time. Working closely with kitchen staff helps us to achieve this goal."

Unit Catering Manager, Julia Underwood

"At Smith's Wood Primary Academy we try to make lunchtime more of an 'experience' by giving the children something to talk and laugh about (it's usually us!). We try to keep the children engaged and interested, and most importantly happy in the dining hall, often dressing up or decorating the serving area, playing music, holding competitions and making pictures from food - this keeps them guessing what ingredients have been used – an important topic of conversation. My team and I work closely with the school to come up with relevant topics that the children are familiar with from their classroom. The variety of ideas keeps it interesting for the catering team too, who all enjoy the light-hearted banter with the younger children.

Having a good team behind me makes my position very enjoyable, I would not be able to organise any of our themes without their extremely hard work and support. It is the best feeling in the world to look up from serving to see the hall full of bubbly children happily eating a healthy meal that they previously may not have chosen.

Our themes are organised in advance and sent out to parents monthly with the daily menu information. Our most recent theme was 'Capital Chaos' – serving menus from Paris, Rome, London and Madrid. I create the letter that is approved and then copied and sent out by the school. This is something that I have taken upon myself to enable the go-ahead with themed and promotional lunches whilst, causing a minimal extra workload to the school office staff. Unit catering managers do not always organise menu information letters home, in most schools this is one of many jobs given to the office staff. This has enabled me to keep in touch with our parents and I use the reverse side to create competitions for the children.

The school has a couple of display boards where parents and children can also find out what is on the menu. Posters are inserted that remind children of future events.

The kitchen team often dress up and sometimes the teaching staff do too. It is lovely to be invited to join in when a special event is happening – we rely on the school teaching staff to keep us informed – and try to carry their themes on into lunchtime as much as possible. These days are always more popular as the children dress up and are more involved too.

I have a good relationship with teaching staff, many of them have school dinners. I ask what topics are coming up soon and many keep me informed of what they are planning. I am always open to suggestions. Not all teachers eat with the children but there are some who do every day. Many topics are repeated and so once it has been organised and followed through the information is there to refer to if it is needed again in the future. Speaking regularly to the staff myself ensures that I get the information that I require.

The lunchtime supervisors give out rewards for good behaviour, they use lunchtime stickers and raffle tickets with prizes to be won each week.

Jamie Oliver has enabled school dinners everywhere to improve. I feel Solihull Catering Services were always supplying healthy meals and that those shown in the media were some of the worst, however since Jamie Oliver's involvement parents, children and catering staff are all more aware of the need for a healthy, balanced meal and menus and recipes are always improving.

I find that children are far more likely to try foods that they otherwise wouldn't when they are served as part of a special day. If a child tries a food and discovers that they actually do like it – we have won! Fruit and vegetables that have been personified are always popular – but then so is the more gruesome food served at Halloween!"

Smith's Wood Primary Academy Tips:

➤ Put a carrier bag on each table so children can put their rubbish into it.
➤ Consider bringing in the Food Dudes – it inspired our work.
➤ Put menu choices on a classroom whiteboard, as they line up children can be given a band for which option they want. So they can go left for hot food, or right for chilled options like filled baguettes with salad.
➤ The unit catering manager comes up with many amazing ideas like encouraging children to learn about rainforests.
➤ See if teachers can have classroom taster session, for example using exotic fruits.
➤ Pilot the noise control "hands up" approach and using golden raffle tickets for talking quietly – many children love this.
➤ See if teachers can sit with the children – can your school offer a free meal if they do?
➤ Look into having Dining Hall Helpers.
➤ Consider having a slow eaters table.

Smith's Wood Primary Academy quotes

From the children

"The dinner is delicious."
"It's cool when the dinner ladies dress up and serve us ever better food."

"The dinners are nice and there is great food every day."
"It looks fantastic!"
"It is amazing trying different things."
"I think it gets the children into a learning mood."

From the catering staff

"Happy! Positive! Friendly! That's how we roll!"
"I'm new to the kitchen team and have never been happier in a job."
"The kitchen is a happy environment because we all work as a team and understand the pressures each and everybody is under. It's helps to have a sense of humour!"
"We will make it fun for the children and we will enjoy it too!"

From a teacher

"The themed lunches provide an enjoyable atmosphere, where the children can further their learning in a fun way."

From a parent

"My son really loves the food he has at school; he loves to sit and eat with his friends and constantly tells me how much choice he has about what he eats, he laughs at some of the 'themed' food and has tried food he wouldn't have at home."

Smith's Wood Primary Academy photographs to inspire you!

All dressed for an Egyptian theme.

Woooo .... Halloween is here – what would you like?

Ghostly and ghastly ... puddings and cakes to celebrate Halloween.

Fabulous puddings! Banana dolphins and popular cartoon characters...

A colourful display of fruit to tempt the children.

Celebrating London on a plate!

Celebrating Paris on a plate!

Celebrating Italy on a plate!

Transport themed food.

Rainforest themed food.

A lovely yellow chick to say spring is here!

This fruity "Fab four" are for display purposes only to encourage the children to eat fruit!

Gorgeous Golden Treasure Cookies!

Another lunchtime experience to shout about from the dining hall rooftops!

Kew Riverside Primary School, Richmond upon Thames

This story concerns an intensively positive, smaller than average primary school in South West London. Now all schools have their challenges and Kew Riverside is no exception. However, there is no doubt to me that this small powerhouse of a school pioneers systems and initiatives that can definitely benefit ALL schools.

To create the dining hall "picture" properly I need to tell you that this school actively champions listening. Listening is at the heart of all they do – and I have been working alongside some of their key staff, including the headteacher, Michael Dillon and class teacher, Sarah Waight for over a period of five years now to help them develop all of their listening systems. The teachers now have in place regular whole group listening – weekly Circle Times, daily "Bubble Time" for children wanting one to one listening and "Think Boxes" are available for all children to put in their worried or their happy thoughts. An integral part of these listening systems is the active support given to the school council and "Playground Leaders." Now, why am I taking up your precious time with these details – what do they have to do with lunchtimes and dining halls? Everything! Children need, at all levels, to feel heard and be responded to.

Schools exist for children – not the other way round!

Listening systems drive a strong beating heart of a school that wants to achieve emotional, social and spiritual wellbeing for all their adults and children. So, naturally, children's needs and hopes drive all of the systems too. In Kew Riverside Primary children have very important jobs as Lunchtime Helpers, they sometimes wear overalls and hair nets (the same as the catering staff). All responsible jobs in the school have to be properly applied for with application forms signed by parents/carers. The children are interviewed before they get their tasks and their uniform – and their training is ongoing.

The children manage the salad bar and actively market and "sell" their wares by encouraging children to make wise choices and try new food. Others take the water to the tables and encourage children to drink up. Another little team talks to the head caterer, Sam, about the food choices that are coming out of the hatch and then with the clipboards they research how the punters respond to it! So when children are about to leave, the researchers come and ask how they feel about the food today. Children LOVE being asked. This feedback then goes back to the kitchen. Other lunchtime helpers sit with young children to help them cut up their food and to encourage them to try new food.

Some years ago, the children, through Circle Time and the school council, insisted that what they wanted more than anything else was to be granted the right to sit anywhere they liked. This they can do. The headteacher, some staff and visitors, will often sit and eat with the children – because the children are PROUD of their dining hall!

I too am so proud of this school that I persuaded them to let me base several of my in-depth "Train the Trainers" courses there. I want all of the delegates to have access to listening to the children and a good lunch experience to refuel them for the afternoon learning.

Headteacher, Michael Dillon

"I think lunchtimes are really successful because we give the children a voice which they know will be listened to and respected. We have children working as lunchtime helpers who get feedback on the menu, help the younger children and look out for positive behaviours from others by rewarding lunchtime lottery tickets. There is a relaxed and calm atmosphere where children have the time to socialise with their friends resulting in a happy school environment."

Class teacher, Sarah Waight

"Lunchtimes at Kew Riverside have always been a special time of the day. It is a relaxed and social experience for all children and staff and we are proud of our achievements. The children come into the dining hall at 12pm starting with Reception and Year 1. The other years come in one class at a time and this is changed on a weekly basis so that no one class is always last or first – this rota is displayed around school and shared with children, staff and parents (although the children seem to have it memorised now and know exactly when it's their turn for lunch).

A bell is rung and a Year 6 Luncthime Helper comes into the playground with a large picture of that class' animal, the children line up and walk into the dining hall. Any child with a packed lunch collects their lunch box and finds a seat and school diners line up at the side. The school menu for that day is displayed at the front of the line, as well as the Year 5 and 6 helpers going along the line and reminding children what there is for lunch that day. In KS1 and Early Years, the class teacher shares with the children what there is for lunch that day before 12pm arrives, this way there are no surprises. Menus are also displayed around school, attached to weekly newsletters and are available to take home from reception, so parents can discuss lunchtimes with their children at home.

A key point of lunchtimes is that children are not told where to sit nor do they have to sit in their year groups or classes. As soon as the children have their lunch they are free to choose their own seat in the hall and may sit with whoever they choose, it is lunchtime after all, not a lesson. This results in Year 6 children sitting with Year 3 children, siblings from different year groups sharing lunch together and an all round mix. Teachers and staff having a school lunch may also sit in the dining hall; our headteacher has a school dinner every day and always sits with the children so he can talk to them.

There is a salad bar run by the lunchtime helpers for children to collect any additional salad or crudités they wish to take to their tables. They do not need to collect cups or knives and forks, as these are already on the table. Each child has a cup of water and the lunchtime helpers come around and fills them up from water jugs when needed. When a child has finished their school dinner they raise their hand to ask if they may eat their dessert – a staff member will ask them to eat more if this is appropriate or allow them to move on to their dessert. Again, the children raise their hand when they have completely finished, checking if it is ok for them to leave the dining hall (this is the same for packed lunches).

There is a designated area of the dining hall for children to clear their plates: putting any food waste into the food recycling bin and plates, cutlery and cups into the washing up section.

Working with the catering staff

There are weekly administration meetings where anything the catering staff want to raise or need to be informed of can be managed. Specific events in school may result in the catering staff putting on special events for lunchtimes. There is clear communication between the admin team and catering staff.

Working with the children to find out what they want

Menus are shared with the children in advance and each day the lunchtime helpers ask a selection of children their opinion on what they are eating.

They are asked to rank the meal from 1-5 and provide any comments they wish to share with our chef. These are then given to him at the end of the week to read and use for future use. In the past this has resulted in certain meals being taken off the menu or added more frequently.

Creating a whole school dining hall policy and having regular meetings

We are very lucky to have all of our TAs working as our lunchtime staff. This results in consistency with the children and solid relationships between staff and pupils. Every week the TAs have a 30 minute meeting where lunchtimes are always part of the agenda. Here they discuss any issues and ways forward with lunchtimes, as well as sharing successes and what has worked well.

Coming up with the idea of children as Lunchtime Helpers

The children play a huge part of our lunchtimes. We have an initiative called "children's roles" where the children apply and are interviewed for certain jobs around the school. One of these jobs is to be a Lunchtime Helper – children who are successful are then given a specific role and responsibility for the year; these include salad bar helpers, collecting the children from the playground and sharing the menu, getting feedback on the food for that day, water monitors and clearing the tables, lunchtime lottery monitors and being a buddy to the younger classes (especially Reception when they first stay for lunch after the October half-term). The children thoroughly enjoy their jobs and take them very seriously.

Lunchtime lottery - a lottery ticket is presented to children who have been following the lunchtime rules in the dining hall and playground. They are given out by lunchtime helpers. In Friday's achievement assembly 2 tickets are chosen at random and the winners receive a prize from the prize box."

Kew Riverside Primary School quotes

School Chef, Richard

"I enjoy being the chef at Kew Riverside Primary School because the children interact with me. I love hearing their news and what they have been learning that day; I can see by their faces that they are happy children. Their opinions matter to me and I want to know if they have enjoyed the food each day, I read their comments and take them on board. Lunchtime feels like an easygoing time and all round nice experience. The older children help the younger children and I can honestly say that when the shutter goes up each day at 12 0'clock we are genuinely happy to see the children."

Teaching assistants working in the dining hall every day

"All the children always remember to use their quiet voices and are very polite, well mannered and sociable. It's an enjoyable time for adults and children to be together."

Lunchtime Helper (Year 6 pupil)

"Lunchtimes are really good! I help the younger children and seeing the look on their faces when they see me coming to help them is fantastic. It's such a lovely feeling putting others before yourself."

Year 4 pupil

"There are loads of different varieties of food and the portions are big! My favourite meal is fish and chips because there's something about the fish that makes it taste special. I like how our opinions matter and we get to decide what we eat, if we don't like something we don't have to eat it again and if we love something we will get to have it again – I really like that."

Year 1 pupils

"You get to talk to your friends and sit next to them."
"It's so light in the dining hall."

What have we learnt from the case studies?

So what have we learnt from the case studies, looking at the dining hall and listening to children and staff?

In the happiest schools:

> ➢ Children love their adults to be enthusiastic about good food.
> ➢ Adults who prepare and serve the food are enthusiastic and sometimes even dress up for the occasion.
> ➢ Teachers know what is going on in the dining hall and support lunchtimes through Circle Time, PSHE, classroom food tasting etc.
> ➢ There are regular meetings where children are involved in the successes of the dining hall from beginning to end, with weekly Circle Times, being able to apply to be a Lunchtime/Dining Hall Helper, or being invited to meetings with the headteacher and dining hall staff.
> ➢ There is a whole school approach – midday supervisors and catering staff are seen as equal to other staff and valued and included in dining hall assemblies; are on the welcome board for parents and mentioned in the school prospectus.
> ➢ The systems are so good that teachers don't need to be there supervising every day.
> ➢ There is evidence that they are dealing with what needs changing and are having a go with new ideas.
> ➢ Love food, love dining, love fun … love learning!

Children love their adults to be enthusiastic about good food.

A note to end on

School meals have been on a real journey of improvement over the last few years. School children deserve the improvements that have been inspired by dedicated and passionate people and organisations who really care about offering children nutritious, tasty, healthy food. It is all going in the right direction.

I notice however in my almost daily work in many different schools, that school dining halls, and the systems used in the dining halls, are often lagging behind all other improvements being made in different areas of the school.

Whether it's the children's behaviour, noise levels, queuing systems or other environmental factors, to get the most out of the dining hall meal experience – these factors can be improved.

In the schools that I have worked in that have already optimised their dining halls and the systems used, it appears that these improvements have a knock-on effect with other aspects of the school. I have seen improvements such as:

➢ Less stressed dining hall staff enjoying their roles and having the energy to help make lunchtimes more creative and fun.
➢ Headteachers and deputies spending less time having to troubleshoot dining hall problems, thus freeing them up to continue with other tasks or even have time to eat their own lunch!
➢ Teaching staff being more positively involved with the dining hall – sharing topics with midday supervisors, holding tasting sessions, sometimes eating in the dining hall and motivating children.
➢ Playtimes after eating lunch are also likely to be a happier time if children have eaten their meals properly with less of the frustrations of long queues and too much noise.

School children deserve the improvements that have been inspired by dedicated and passionate people and organisations who really care about offering children nutritious, tasty, healthy food.

Playtimes after eating lunch are also likely to be a happier time if children have eaten their meals properly with less of the frustrations of long queues and too much noise.

➢ Children going back to the classroom for an afternoon of focus and learning which is a goal for all of us!

So in some ways the dining hall can be thought of as a missing link between excellent classroom practice, fabulous healthy lunches and improved playtimes.

So in some ways the dining hall can be thought of as a missing link between excellent classroom practice, fabulous healthy lunches and improved playtimes.

Useful organisations

Allergy UK	www.allergyuk.org
CED Trade Supplies	www.cedtrade.co.uk
Change 4 Life	www.nhs.uk/change4life
Children's Food Trust	www.childrensfoodtrust.org.uk
Coeliac UK	www.coeliac.org.uk/schools
Food Dudes	www.fooddudes.co.uk
Food for Life Partnership/ Jeanette Orrey	www.foodforlife.org.uk
Jamie Oliver	www.jamieoliver.com
National Health Education Group (NHEG)	www.nheg.org.uk
PSHE Association	www.pshe-association.org.uk
Soil Association	www.soilassociation.org
School Food Matters	www.schoolfoodmatters.com
School Food Plan	www.schoolfoodplan.com

References

Belot, M and James, J, (2009). "Healthy School Meals and Educational Outcomes", Institute for Social and Economic Research, Paper 2009-1

Brooks, F, (2013). Chapter 7: Life stage: School Years, in Chief Medical Officer's annual report 2012: Our Children Deserve Better: Prevention Pays, ed. Professor Dame Sally C Davies. London: DH

Department for Education (2013), The national curriculum in England Framework document www.gov.uk/government/uploads/system/uploads/attachment_data/file/210969/NC_framework_document_-_FINAL.pdf

Dimbleby, H and Vincent, J (2013). The School Food Plan Available online at: http://www.schoolfoodplan.com/wp-content/uploads/2013/07/School_Food_Plan_2013.pdf

Food Dudes, (2014). From website www.fooddudes.co.uk

London Economics. (2008). Estimating the econimic impact of healthy eating. Available: http://www.childrensfoodtrust.org.uk/research/economics/economic-case. Last accessed June 2015.

Ofsted, (2013). The framework for school inspection. From website www.ofted.gov.uk

Ofsted, (2014). The framework for school inspection From website www.ofsted.gov.uk

Oliver, J, (2011). Jamie's Manifesto (Part II) Recommendations to the Government School Food Policy Review. From website www.jamieoliver.com

School Food Trust, (2010). A Fresh Look at the School Meal Experience, 2nd edition, SFT

Weichselbaum, E and Buttriss, J, (2014) Diet, nutrition and schoolchildren: an update. Nutrition Bulletin, DOI: 10.1111/nbu.12071. The paper is available for free on the Wiley Blackwell Website: www.onlinelibrary.wiley.com/doi/10.1111/nbu.12071/abstract

Training and resources

Resources

Resources can help your initiatives come to life. A poster on the dining hall wall can speak up for you when you are busy working in other areas. We have carefully designed resources especially for schools, all of which are displayed in our catalogue and on our website. Some of our most relevant resources are:

- Golden Rules poster
- Dining Hall Rules poster
- High Five "We have good manners in the dining hall" poster
- A3 dining hall posters
- Dining hall stickers

All resources can be ordered through the Positive Press shop at www.circle-time.co.uk or call 01225 719204 for a full catalogue.

You will find a selection of photocopiable resources in Appendix 2 at the end of this book and on the accompanying CD-ROM.

Training available from Jenny Mosley Consultancies

Areas of expertise:

- Powerfully Positive Lunchtimes and Playtimes – helping to create calm, positive and productive lunchtimes and playtimes, so children return to their classroom activities calm, happy and ready to play and learn.
- Quality Circle Time – a whole school approach to improving social skills, communication skills and emotional literacy whilst valuing individuals.
- Positive Behaviour for Learning – uniting everyone in a consistent vision, using tried and tested positive behaviour management techniques.
- Looking after the emotional health, wellbeing and energy

of all staff – your number one asset!

➤ Specially designed training days and workshops for parents, teaching assistants, learning mentors, midday supervisors and all adults in school.

Training options

➤ Open conferences – throughout the country, throughout the year, we hold open workshops for teachers, managers, MDSAs and LSAs to book places on. Courses are for Better Behaviour for Learning, Powerfully Positive Lunchtimes and Early Years.

➤ INSET closure day – with all adults, designed to meet current needs.

➤ Cluster Conference Days – large groups from different schools.

➤ Working in School Days – a non-closure day where Jenny trains staff and holds demonstrations in the classroom, playground and staff room.

➤ Training packages – combinations of the different types of training days to help bring transformation.

➤ Train the Trainers – in-depth accredited Quality Circle Time training for staff wishing introduce new systems to their school or setting and to train others.

➤ Partnership projects – longer training projects for funded partnerships using grant funding and addressing particular issues of local or national concern.

Who is our training for?

➤ Headteachers, teachers, teaching assistants.
➤ Midday supervisors, lunchtime supervisors, MDSAs, SENCOs, early years practitioners, advisors etc.
➤ Parents or carers … depending upon the course.

For more information about training and resources:
Call: 01225 767157
Email: circletime@jennymosley.co.uk
Website: www.circle-time.co.uk

Appendix 1

Photocopiable dining hall questionnaires

QUESTIONS FOR HEADTEACHERS

We are looking at ways of improving the dining experience for all our children and would be grateful if you would give your views on the following questions.

What is not working well in your dining hall?	
Can you list three things that work well with your lunchtimes and dining halls?	
Are you having to spend a large part of every day in the dining hall helping out?	
Have "Universal infant free school meals" tipped the balance into chaos?	
Have you noticed some children not eating?	
Are there comments from parents or staff about children crying at lunchtime?	
Is there enough time for the children to sit and eat?	
How is your dining hall organised and is there anything in the physical environment that you can see not working?	
Do teachers release the children on time from class so that lunchtimes run smoothly?	
How are children promptly dismissed after eating?	
Do children put their hands up and then their plates or lunch boxes are checked to ensure they have eaten enough?	
Could your school afford to give teachers a free school meal if they sit and eat with the children?	
Do your kitchen catering staff and midday supervisors have meetings and work together as a good team?	
Is there time for dining hall supervisors to talk to a senior midday supervisor or teachers about their concerns regarding some children's eating problems?	
Any other comments?	

QUESTIONS FOR TEACHERS AND TEACHING ASSISTANTS NOT INVOLVED IN THE DINING HALL

We are looking at ways of improving the dining experience for all our children and would be grateful if you would give your views on the following questions.	
What do children complain most about to do with their dining halls and lunchtimes?	
Have you ever gone into the dining hall to see how your children are responding?	
Have the dining hall supervisors ever talked to you about children in your class not eating well or having any food problems?	
Have you, in any staff meetings, ever discussed the dining hall?	
Have you ever done any PSHE sessions on food, eating and the dining experience with your class?	
Do you discuss the menu options with the children before lunchtime?	
Do you ever show children pictures of the food, so they can choose their meals in advance?	
Are you aware of the research on children eating well and the link to their learning?	
Do you and parents/carers communicate with each other about eating at school?	
What is currently working well for your children and the dining hall and eating experience?	

Can you write anything else about lunchtimes?

QUESTIONS FOR CATERING STAFF AND MIDDAY SUPERVISORS

Given that most schools have to follow strict guidelines and work with the county council on what is offered to children in the dining hall, we are limited in what we can and cannot change about the lunchtime systems. Nevertheless, we are really keen to try and improve the dining hall experience within the constraints we might have and would value your feedback.

Are you happy with the "look" of the dining hall?	
Do you find the queues are too long?	
Are you ever given a chance to be creative with food?	
How do you find the time to make things extra special in the dining hall?	
Are you aware of any themes of the term that you might be able to tie in with your own ideas?	
Do you think the children speak respectfully to you – with please and thank you?	
Are there Dining Hall Rules up in the dining hall?	
Do you know what the Dining Hall Rules are off by heart?	
Do you have meetings with your headteacher?	
Are you invited to any school events?	
What are noise levels like in the dining hall?	
Does the noise in the dining hall stop you from hearing the children's voices?	
What do you do when it gets too loud and noisy and when somebody needs to make an announcement?	
Have you ever been encouraged to use the "hands up" approach to ask for quiet?	
Do you think the children know their choices when they enter the hall and can they all make their choices easily (even the youngest)?	
Are you given any rewards, incentives or stickers to hand out to the children?	
How do you help slow eaters?	
Do you have a slow eaters table that they can go on to finish their meal?	
Do you have any system for how children should leave the dining hall – do they put their hand up for you to check their plate?	
Is there a lot of mess on and under the tables?	

Do you have a system for scraping the plates and does it work well?	
Have you tried the "Golden Table of the Week" for children who keep the dining hall rules?	
Do you ever have meetings with the other dining hall staff and yourself?	
Have you ever been invited to assemblies about the dining hall and how to make it happier?	
Do you have regular meetings with the catering team and senior managers together about the dining hall?	
How do you motivate your staff team?	
Do children ever complain to you about anything to do with the dining hall and food?	
Do you have a chance to speak to teachers about the children and their behaviour or eating?	
If you're ever worried about a child not eating who do you take this worry to?	
How do you find out about children's special dietary needs or issues – is it by talking to their teacher?	
What have you put in place recently that works well?	
Can you write anything else about lunchtimes?	

QUESTIONS FOR PUPILS WHO HAVE SCHOOL MEALS

	YES	NO	SOMETIMES
Do you like the school meals at your school?			
Do you always get the choices that you want?			
When you choose your meal in the morning, do you understand what the choices are?			
Are you happy with where you sit for lunch?			
Has a grown-up ever sat at your table to eat with you?			
When you've finished your food do you put your hand up to wait for someone to check your plate?			
If you are waiting for a supervisor does he/she come quickly?			
Do you always finish your food?			
Do you scrape your plate yourself or does someone else do it?			
Is there usually a lot of mess on or under your table?			
Is the noise all right or is it too loud in the dining hall?			
How does it make you feel if noise in the dining hall is too loud?			
Do you queue for too long to get your food?			
Do you ever have stickers or anything for trying new food or for being quiet and tidy?			
Have you ever been on a "Golden Table of the Week"?			
If people are naughty at lunchtimes what happens?			
Can you write anything else about lunchtimes?			

*Younger children can be asked the questions during a Circle Time and their responses written down by someone.

QUESTIONS FOR PUPILS WHO HAVE PACKED LUNCHES

	YES	NO	SOMETIMES
Do you like having a packed lunch at school?			
Do you have some healthy food in your lunch box like some fruit or vegetables?			
Do you have treats in your lunch box like sweets, chocolate or crisps in your lunch box?			
Does a teacher or midday supervisor check what is in your lunch box?			
Are you happy with where you sit for lunch?			
Do grown-ups sometimes eat with you at your table?			
When you've finished your food do you put your hand up to wait for someone to check your lunch box?			
Do you put all your rubbish in the bin?			
Is there usually a lot of mess on your table or under it?			
Is the noise all right in the dining hall?			
Do you ever have stickers, or anything else, for being quiet, polite or tidy?			

Can you write anything else about lunchtimes?

QUESTIONS FOR PARENTS

Given that most schools have to follow strict guidelines and work with the county council on what is offered to children in the dining hall, we are limited in what we can and cannot change about the lunchtime systems. Nevertheless, we are really keen to try and improve the dining hall experience within the constraints we might have and would value your feedback.

Do your children ever talk about the dining hall and the food they are offered?	
Do you get menus sent home and do you have time to talk through the options with your child?	
If your child is going through a funny stage about certain foods, have you ever written a letter, or talked to the teacher about it?	
Are you aware that your child has salad choices? Do your children know what "5 A DAY" means and the importance of fruit and vegetables?	
If your child has a packed lunch, do you feel happy to know they have eaten their food or do you like them to bring wrappers back to show you what they have eaten?	
Has your child ever talked about cookery, taster sessions or growing projects?	
Has your child's teacher ever talked about your child's eating at school?	
In the school brochure is there anything about "healthy eating" and/or what the school dining hall offers?	

Is there anything else you would like to tell us about lunchtimes?

Appendix 2

Photocopiable dining hall resources

OUR DINING HALL RULES...

We line up calmly.

We walk carefully through the dining hall.

We are polite to everyone.

We speak quietly to those around us.

We use good table manners.

We keep our table clean.

We clean our plate tidily.

Dear ....

You have kept all of the Dining Hall Rules and are invited to sit at our Golden Table next week.

Signed ....

Dear ....

You have kept all of the Dining Hall Rules and are invited to sit at our Golden Table next week.

Signed ....

Thank you

for lining up calmly.

signed.........................

Thank you

for lining up calmly.

signed.........................

Thank you

for being polite
to everyone.

signed............................

Thank you

for being polite
to everyone.

signed............................

Thank you

for trying some
new food today.

signed......................................

© 2014 Jenny Mosley

Thank you

for trying some
new food today.

signed......................................

© 2014 Jenny Mosley

Thank you

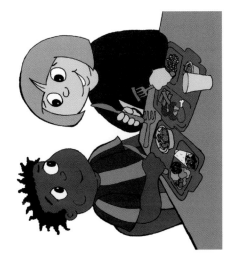

for using good table manners.

signed.......................................

Thank you

for using good table manners.

signed.......................................

Thank you

for speaking quietly.

signed..

Thank you

for speaking quietly.

signed..

Thank you

for finishing your
lunch today.

signed..

Thank you

for finishing your
lunch today.

signed..

Thank you

for keeping the
table clean.

signed......................................

Thank you

for keeping the
table clean.

signed......................................

How to create calm dining halls

Thank you

for cleaning your plate tidily.

signed...

© 2014 Jenny Mosley

Thank you

for cleaning your plate tidily.

signed...

© 2014 Jenny Mosley

Thank you

for walking carefully.

signed..

Thank you

for walking carefully.

signed..

How to create calm dining halls

DINING HALL CERTIFICATE

CONGRATULATIONS! YOU HAVE...

Lined up calmly

Walked carefully through the dining hall

Been polite to everyone

Spoken quietly to those around you

Used good table manners

Kept your table clean

Cleaned your plate tidily

Tried new food

Finished all your lunch

signed.......................................

© 2014 Jenny Mosley PHOTOCOPIABLE FOR PERSONAL USE ONLY.

DINING HALL CERTIFICATE

CONGRATULATIONS! YOU HAVE...

Lined up calmly

Walked carefully through the dining hall

Been polite to everyone

Spoken quietly to those around you

Used good table manners

Kept your table clean

Cleaned your plate tidily

Tried new food

Finished all your lunch

signed.......................................

© 2014 Jenny Mosley PHOTOCOPIABLE FOR PERSONAL USE ONLY.

I am really HAPPY with you because you chose to:

1. Line up calmly
2. Walk carefully through the hall
3. Be polite to everyone
4. Speak quietly to those around you

5. Use good table manners
6. Keep your table clean
7. Clean your plate tidily

You have kept the Dining Hall Rules.

Name .... Class ....

Supervisor .... Date...............

I am really HAPPY with you because you chose to:

1. Line up calmly
2. Walk carefully through the hall
3. Be polite to everyone
4. Speak quietly to those around you

5. Use good table manners
6. Keep your table clean
7. Clean your plate tidily

You have kept the Dining Hall Rules.

Name .... Class ....

Supervisor .... Date...............

I am SAD that having quietly warned you, you still chose NOT to:

1. Line up calmly
2. Walk carefully through the hall
3. Be polite to everyone
4. Speak quietly to those around you
5. Use good table manners
6. Keep your table clean
7. Clean your plate tidily

Name .... Class ....

Supervisor .... Date..............

I am SAD that having quietly warned you, you still chose NOT to:

1. Line up calmly
2. Walk carefully through the hall
3. Be polite to everyone
4. Speak quietly to those around you
5. Use good table manners
6. Keep your table clean
7. Clean your plate tidily

Name .... Class ....

Supervisor .... Date..............

DINING HALL HELPER – APPLICATION FORM

I would like to be considered for the role of Dining Hall Helper and agree to be a role model to the other children and to help them keep the Dining Hall Rules – which are:

- We line up calmly.
- We walk carefully through the dining hall.
- We are polite to everyone.
- We speak quietly to those around us.
- We use good table manners.
- We keep our table clean.
- We clean our plate tidily.

Please tick the tasks that you would be interested in doing in the table below.

Task	Tick if you would like to do this
Bringing in children from outside to have their lunch.	
Preparing the tables. This might include laying a table with a cloth, cutlery, glasses and water.	
Helping younger children with choosing their meal.	
Helping children to find a seat and cutting up the food of younger children or showing them how to do it.	
Serving salad or other cold meals (Health and Hygiene rules apply).	
Refilling water jugs throughout the meal times.	
Walking around the dining hall and prompting diners to pick up dropped items and clear away rubbish before they leave the dining hall.	
Helping diners, especially younger children, to clear away their plates and cutlery.	
Being available to run errands and carry out jobs for lunchtime staff.	

Name ....

Print name ....

Parent/carer signature .... Date ....

FOR OFFICE USE ONLY

Application approved by .... Date ....

DINING HALL HELPER
CERTIFICATE OF APPRECIATION

This certificate has been awarded to

....

*for being an outstanding
Dining Hall Helper
and for keeping the dining hall
calm and happy for everyone!*

THANK YOU!

Signed ....

Print name ....

Date...